CW00495021

My Dad
Was
The King of Clubs

By

Scott Stringfellow

UNBOUND
PUBLISHING

MEDIA

© **Copyright 2020, Unbound Publishing, LLC., Ida-**
ho, United States of America, and Scott Stringfellow.
Produced under a cooperative agreement with Agent Fox
Media, London. All rights Reserved.

No part of this publication may be reproduced, stored in a retrieval system, or transmitted in any form or by any means, electronic, mechanical, photocopying, recording, scanning, or otherwise, without the prior written permission of the author.

Unbound Publishing is committed to publishing works of quality and integrity. In that spirit, we are proud to offer this book to our readers; however, the story, the experiences, and the words are the author's alone. Some individuals mentioned in the book may have different memories, as they experienced this story from another point of view. The conversations in the book all come from the author's recollections, though they are not written to represent word-for-word transcripts. Rather, the author has retold them in a way that evokes the feeling and meaning what was said and in all instances, the essence of the dialogue is accurate.

Contents

Acknowledgements:

I'd like to thank Rick & Beverley Mayston at Agent Fox Media and Mick Mamuzelos, our cover designer, here in GB.

Troy Lambert, Jerry Mooney, and everyone on the team at Unbound publishing over in the US for all their hard work in getting this book to see the light of day.

Sean Driscoll for getting me in touch with Agent Fox MEDIA in the first place.

The many friends from Facebook who when I mentioned my writing also encouraged me to keep at it.

Richard Dean for being a great friend over the years.

Peter Harris who has been my wingman and best friend in the BTCC safety car for over 15 years, who also kept me together when things got tough after the loss of my dad.

My Mum Coral needs a special mention as she was also a great help with some aspects to do with years and some details that helped jog my memory, and of course was a part of the story too.

All my friends that are a part of the British Touring Cars Championship who understood where my mind was at when I turned up for work after losing dad, they have no idea how much it helped me to be on track with my beloved safety cars, particularly at Oulton Park. Alan Gow, Ian Watson, Dan Mayo, Dr. Paul Trafford and Alan Hyde you were all so gracious and kind to understand how much I needed to be at the track.

The councillors at MIND in Aylesbury for helping me back into the light when the world seemed at its darkest. Bereavement Counselling is a great help to anyone who needs a helping hand. I highly recommend it.

My thanks also to Karen and Bella, we were a team at the hospital during the hardest time of our lives.

To my ex-wife Sophy who has also been so supportive through the hardest times after the loss.

Finally to my dad for being an outstanding Father, friend and human being. Having the opportunity to live my dream is something many people don't get the privilege to do. Without him it would all have been a lot harder. And I'm glad I got to thank him in the hospital while he was still with us. Also to work alongside him was a complete education that was filled with golden moments and advice that nobody could replicate.

I dedicate this book to my father who gave me so many opportunities and never stepped on my dreams. Also to my children who grew up having fun with their Pop-pop, and now they can read about my life with him. I'd also like to include my half-sister Karen who grew up right alongside me, we were both very lucky to have him.

FOREWORD

What follows is a straightforward account of life with my dad, though he was known as the King of Clubs, he was still just my dad to me.

Everyone in the world loses their parents eventually, either to illness, accident or just plain old age. It ranks highly in the list of most traumatic events in all our lives. Remembering your parents is important, the good times and the bad. Some people have had terrible parents. Some people are orphaned and grow up with or without surrogate parents. Some people, like me, have great parents.

The title "celebrity" has been around for as long as anyone can remember, and those who are considered as such, come in all types of jobs, but all are known because of television, radio or the press, and more recently... the internet! In short, they are covered under the term "the media".

Some "celebs" can't cope with the attention, and some know how to use it to their advantage.

My dad was very good at being a celeb. He was just known enough to be well known, but not so well known to subject him to being hounded by the press and cameras.

The loss of my dad was huge, and the life I had with him was different, I guess, to most people. So here it is... We start at the end and go back to the beginning.

This is life with Peter Stringfellow through a son's eyes.

1

Blowing out the Candles

Everyone has a point where something happens in life that changes everything. It's an apt description "the twists and turns of life".

My personal curveball came along in 2017.

Mid-December 2017… Out of the blue my phone rings…

It's my dad's wife, Bella (his 3rd). She lets me know he has become unwell. He's experiencing sudden coldness and shivering, he has had a brush with cancer twice, he has to be careful now whenever he gets even slightly ill. When you have one and a half lungs and half your stomach missing, you take no chances. He went into hospital, not a local one, but the one in London. He went to that one as he'd had an op on his bile duct in the summer of 2017, and that was his second attempt of cancer, the first was in 2008 with his lung. He didn't even smoke and was not a fan of anyone else doing it.

On this occasion it was a suspected infection. But tests were carried out, and yes it was an infection, of the liver this time. But there was a blockage in the bile duct again, and a "procedure" was called for. That's hospital speak for another operation.

We were all happy that this was going to happen, and looked forward to him coming out again pretty soon… But this time it was found to be something more….

Terminal isn't a word you want to hear unless it's the location of where your plane is on holiday.

Worse still, they gave him a timescale. 6 to 18 months.

When they told my dad, he went into mild shock. Who wouldn't? According to Bella, he started shaking uncontrollably, but after a little while he calmed… though still struggling with the news. He was a tough guy, but I have no doubt in my mind that his thoughts went straight to my little brother and sister. My elder sister and I are in our 50s, but we also have a younger brother and sister, at this time they were 2 and 4 years old. They were about to lose their father way too young. For Bella to explain this one was going to be very tough.

When the phone call about the updated news came to me, I could tell straight away by her voice it wasn't good. Coincidentally my mother was down to stay with me for Christmas and my upcoming birthday. I took a little stroll away from her in the kitchen, which is where I took the call. I decided to go to my bedroom, which was well out of earshot.

Bella filled me in on the details as I walked, and just as I got in my room, the word "terminal" was used. It stopped me cold in my tracks. I was ready for news that the big C was back, but nothing that was final, or had an expiry date attached to it. It could be as much as a year and a half or game over by the summer!

It was like being hit with a sledgehammer, I suppose. I felt dizzy, upset, and started shaking a bit myself. I just sat on my bed looking out of the window staring at nothing… I managed to compose myself enough to finish the conversation. After I finished talking to Bella, I just sat there for about 2 minutes and realised the terrible truth that I was going to have to tell my mum.

The walk down my two flights of stairs felt surreal, and by the time I got back to the kitchen where she was, the shakes were back. I walked round the table and sat opposite her. She could see straight away what I was about to say wasn't good. I didn't do any drawn out speech, I just told her how it was.

My mum and Dad had been divorced for something like 27 years but had split up 2 years previous to that. Though they had not seen each other for quite a few years, they were married for 23 years previous to the divorce. It was still a lot of time together. And if you do the maths, I was at their wedding too. The point is, my mum felt the pain of the news just as I did.

She instantly started to cry, if anything more for me than herself. And at this point I let go some of my composure. Life was about to get very hard, and 2018 was only 2 days away. My sister over in America was informed, and she too fell apart, and was on the next flight over to be there for our dad.

New Year's Eve was a strange affair. 2017 had finished with a sting in the tail, and 2018 was going to prolong it. It was into the new year that something else was rearing its painful head. We had already lost my dad's next brother, Geoff, to Alzheimer's, which was painful for my dad. His other brother, Paul had been fighting cancer himself, and into the second week into the new year, he was losing the battle. He literally had days left, and dad managed to go see him, once he had got the go ahead from the hospital. And just a couple of days later, he was gone.

The day he died I had just been away for the day to visit the Autosport Racing Car show. It's like an annual pilgrimage for motorsport heads to gather. I went to get my head out of the hospital life, take a break, I guess. I'd had a nice time, saw people I knew, and saw a lot of cars that were interesting.

When I got home in the evening, and on my own, I had a moment or two of feeling very upset about everything. I was on the verge of tears watching something on TV because my mind had wandered, and I felt very sad. But I got myself together and went to bed, where I struggled to get to sleep. It took a whiskey to help me…. I'd better not let that become a regular thing.

In the morning, I had a text message from dad. Paul had passed away in the night surrounded by his family at home. A nice end for a very nice guy.

Dad was philosophical when I spoke to him later in the day, we all knew the end was close for Paul, yet it was still a bit of a shock. Paul had been a fixture at the club from the early days. Even though he had been a roadie for a little while for Jimi Hendrix and the Eagles.

Paul became bar's manager for most of dad's clubs until we moved to London, but by that point dad's other brother Geoff opened his own club/bar in Manchester. Paul worked there for a bit until that closed too. Dad then brought Paul down to London and placed him as bars manager there until the end of Paul's life, 35 years.

I liked my Uncle Paul a lot. He was my favourite Uncle. He was straight, funny and a kind man. He didn't seek fame or fortune; he just enjoyed life. Though, he did do a little DJ'ing at our Leeds clubs Cinderella's & Rockerfella's. I still have the tape somewhere from a Christmas night.

* * *

My dad's situation was going to be a frustrating one. For now, he had to wait a little as his scars from the last procedure healed before they could do more surgery. But he was due to start heavy chemotherapy. He had chosen the heavy dose route hoping to reduce the tumour and give him more time on earth.

It took time to get started as he also contracted an infection that came when he had stents fitted. But once that was dealt with, he got the clearance to go home. He had a small relapse and ended up staying at the hospital right up to the first dose of chemo.

At this time, I myself developed a cough and cold, so I couldn't go see him for a while. Once that cleared off, Karen, Bella and I started taking it in turns staying overnight at the hospital with him, we were constant, playing hospital tag. He was never going to be on his own. The Princess Grace hospital was not far from where we used to live in London many years before; literally less than 500 yards from our front door. It was a surreal situation for Karen and me, which was something Bella couldn't expect to feel with us.

My mum came down to spend some time with me and the kids for a bit, which was also nice to have her around again while all this was going on. One time she had to come to the hospital with me, and though she had the chance, she decided not to see dad. It was hard for her, but she wanted to remember him as she remembered him, and not in whatever state he was now in. And as hard as that was, it was the right thing to do.

I told dad about mum, and he totally got it. But it must have been hard for him too, as even though they had not seen each other for years, they spent a large part of their lives together.

The days dragged on. I developed a routine with him as he slowly deteriorated, I would feed him, and later in the evening before settling down to sleep I would play him 60s music on my iPhone. It was great, and something I would never forget. We did The Kinks, some Motown, the Stones, and of course The Beatles.

The room he was in had its own toilet and shower. In the corner sat a strange shaped chair that converted into a single bed where I slept, and I used to just lay there listening to him breathing in the dark after lights out. I was happy as long as he was breathing. There were other noises, like alarms from other rooms when a nurse was called, and also the chattering from nurses at the main station, which wasn't far away from his room.

The routine was set, give him his breakfast, help him to the loo after he threw back his covers, saying, "I need to pee". I'd chat with him, and get some very interesting information, he would watch a bit of TV, I would read, then either Bella, Karen or my dad's PA Pat would relieve me of my shift. Then I'd go find breakfast myself.

As the days wore on, his eating habits were getting more limited, and he was favouring things that were easier for him to eat including Porridge and ice cream. It was as yet another sign of his slow deterioration. His trips to the loo came to an end as his strength weakened, and the docs decided it was time to fit a catheter.

Dad would still throw the covers back a bit and say, "I need to pee," and hold his hands out for helping him up. I had to explain to him that now he had a catheter he didn't have to leave the bed, and the same with other stuff too… He didn't cope with that too well at first. I think he found it quite degrading and another sign he was losing his independence.

In time, he got over that as he got worse. The orderlies would come in and turn him in his bed and fit new sheets around him, I would help with moving him if I was there as more hands helped the whole thing move along quicker. The nurses and orderlies were fantastic, very caring and respectful. And very quick but gentle when dealing with my dad, and I'm sure with everyone else who occupied a bed in that ward.

It was incredibly hard to see the slow disintegration of a clever, brave man, who had been my loving dad for 52 years.

On the 3rd of June, a Sunday morning, I could see he had really slowed down on eating breakfast, I was feeding him, and also not wanting so much on the spoon. I knew then we were getting close to losing him. I felt sick. It's like watching a film and knowing its nearly the end, and its building up to a sad ending. The next couple of days got harder, he spoke less, ate less, and was generally slipping away in front of my eyes. I dreaded going in for my shift, but also hated the thought I would get a phone call while I was away. I knew it was going to be this week.

During this terrible time, my Dad's youngest brother Terry passed away, he was in another hospital with his own problems with obesity and the alcoholism that got him that way. We had decided not to say anything as Dad was having his own hard time, but if he asked, we would clue him in.

I didn't feel comfortable with that, as dad always liked to be the one to know how everyone was. But on one of my shifts a day or two later, Dad was trying to say something. I was in the room on my own with him, just reading a book while he slipped in and out of sleep. But he looked like he was trying to say something, and one word came out… "Brother." I lowered my book looked at him, and carefully said, "Are you asking about Terry Dad?"

His reply, "… yes…"

Ok, this was it… "I'm Sorry, Dad, but Terry passed away last Friday (we were now into Monday).

He had no energy for any big reaction, just, "Oh, dear!"

I told him that I wanted to tell him when it happened, but we felt he had enough to deal with, but only if he asked would we let him know.

He gave a slight smile; I think he understood we were just thinking of him.

Frankly, I was relieved to get it out of my mind. I was going to go to the funeral later in the week to represent him, as I didn't get on with Terry at all, but for Dad, I would go.

We were told that one of the signs of the time being very near was a marked change in his breathing pattern, and they were not wrong. Wednesday the 6th of June came, and it started. And by this time, he had been moved to another room, a much bigger one farther away from the reception desk. It was much quieter, and though we could still hear the odd room alarm calls going off from time to time, they were not so intrusive. That or we just got used to it. Also, with this room we could fit three funny bed chairs, so we could all stay with him. So, we were all right beside him, and we would take the odd personal break out of the room as the whole situation was heart-breaking.

The evening came, he'd not spoken for 2 days straight, and was not moving, just a strange rhythmic breathing with long breaths. As night came, we all settled in, but there was a different feeling in the room. I think we all knew the end was imminent.

Bella was on dads' bed right next to him, Karen and I were on our single beds, we were just lying there listening to his breathing willing him to keep going.

It was about this time that a song kept coming into my head, but as I was stressing about what was happening, I couldn't get what it was. I took some time out of the room to call my mum and bring her up to speed on events. She asked me that when the time comes, and I decide when to call her again, don't say he's died... say something else.

I promised I would, but no idea what I would say! I then called my wife, and even though we were separated we still got on well. She gave me an idea about what to say to mum as she reminded me that my mum had got dad a birthday present many years ago, of a star in the sky somewhere named after him.

I went back to the room and eventually fell asleep.

At some point in the early hours, Karen woke me and said, "Scott, we think it's nearly time, do you want to be awake for it?"

I thought it was a strange ask, but then again, people can say funny things when they don't really know what else to say.

I took up station at the foot of the bed with Karen next to dad on his right, and Bella on his left. I couldn't stop looking at the pulse in his neck, I became quite fixated, I just didn't want him to end… he made some strange involuntary movements with his arms, I suddenly remembered my mum telling me this happened to her mum just before she passed away. So, I knew it really was it… And then that song in my head came back, and this time I knew what it was. The Phil Collins version of "A groovy kind of love."

I had no idea why it was on repeat in my head, but there it was.

He seemed to relax. The breaths got longer until, without any drama he just stopped breathing.

For some crazy reason, I took note of the time. 4:01am on the 7th of June, the King of Clubs, my dad… passed away.

The date was significant for a couple of other reasons. It was my nephew Taylor's, Karen's son's, birthday, which will forever be hard for my sister. Also, it was the day of my uncle Terry's funeral, which I was meant to go to. But that certainly wasn't going to happen.

Effectively our worlds stood still.

After a little time of getting ourselves together… I went to call my mum. I told her, "Dad has gone to find the star you got for him, mum!"

Then at 6:00 a.m. we let the press release go about his passing. Within three minutes, I got my first text of sympathy, and from that moment on, it didn't stop all day.

While we were allowed back in the room to be with him after they made him more presentable, the news was on the TV in the room... SKY News was full of the news about my dad. That I can tell you is surreal, and in a strange way annoying. I didn't want the world into our grief like that.

Dad looked serene, and empty. All I could think was... he's not in there anymore.

It was a strange thing, but we all left the hospital eventually...

I had driven into London. I rationalised that I'd rather drive home shell shocked rather than sit on a train with other strangers around me. But on my way to my car, I decided to sit in Regents Park, this was at the back of where we used to live, and it was a lovely sunny day.

I found an unoccupied park bench, sat down, and started thinking about the past with dad.

So, I'm going to take you back to my earliest recollections of my life with dad, a life that was filled with wonderful times and a side of the man you never knew, but who I grew up with.

2

YOU MUST BE DADDY
(SHEFFIELD-LEEDS)

My earliest recollections of my dad are a little unsure, because like most children in general, my mum was my main memory. I was born in 1966, but my parents were in a sticky social situation, my dad was married to someone else when he met my mum and had me before they themselves were married to each other. Actually, I was at the wedding. I remember we were in a small house in Sheffield, which is where I was born.

I hear my dad wasn't at my birth. I've been told he was at the office at his club "The King Mojo." No mobiles back then, and he was unaware until he rang my mum's mother asking how she was doing, and he was met with the words "she is in hospital having YOUR child!"

My grandmother didn't mince her words.

Dad dashed down in the evening and was overjoyed with seeing the bundle of baby boy before him.

I must have been about 3 or 4 when I remember seeing dad from time to time, and I have a picture from the time we were in that small house, of him on the sofa asleep with his club gear on.

Dad's success in clubs or dance halls was sparked off by him taking on a turn called The Beatles in 1963, whom he paid far more for than any other act at that time. Demand was so great for tickets that he had to hire the Sheffield Azena Ballroom, as his club couldn't take the crowd.

It was the first time he made a substantial profit. This one event catapulted dad's reputation in Sheffield and in the north so much that people were attracted to come enjoy his own club. He started booking some really good bands and singers and opened his doors to some of the new acts coming over from America, like Ike & Tina Turner, Little Stevie Wonder and also other acts like John Mayall's Blues Breakers when they had Eric Clapton in the band.

He worked hard, booking the forthcoming acts together with his brother Geoff, then headed back home later in the day to have a pre-work sleep before getting into his clubbing clothes and off to work. His mother and father were involved with the club too. His mum Elsie was on the door taking the entry fee, and his dad Jim, a doorman! This was what I saw from the very beginning, my dad worked nights, I don't think I ever had breakfast with him, except when we went on holiday.

As for my perceptions of dad at an early age... I thought maybe he was a singer? Which, in fact, he did have a go at. Well, I think he wanted to be a singer, he even did a couple of demo songs. My mother has a couple of scratchy singles he did. But as the club life got better, he put that idea behind him.

Before all the club stuff started, he had done some very "normal" jobs. He was a shoe salesman for about half a day. He worked for a bakery for a while, and even learned to drive in the bread van. He really got into working for a carpet sales company. Dobson's, I think it was called. He had a van and a small team of girls who helped on the sales when they went out to deliver or show their products in someone's home.

Along the way, he found they had a fair number of off cuts, and some that would do very nicely for small spaces. And so, he took the idea that he could sell these bits that weren't needed and make a little profit on the side. He genuinely thought this was okay, until someone he was dealing with turned out to be an undercover policeman. The firm wanted to know what was happening to their excess stock. When they found out, they put my dad away in prison for a couple of months for it.

Though that sounds bad, my dad used to say it was probably one of the best things that happened to him in life. Because the judge listened to his story and described dad as a "glib" young man. Dad thought it was a compliment until he looked it up. And then they put him in a cell with an "old lag" as the lifers were known.

The guy really took dad under his wing and told him straight, that trying to be smart and stealing was a mugs' game. My dad respected his elders and took the guy's words to heart. He came out early for good behaviour. He made his mind up to find work and not get involved with anything dodgy again.

A close friend of my dad's took him to a dance hall that was playing the latest music, somewhere further up north, and he saw a room full of kids around his age packing the room out and were dancing away like crazy to the rock n roll music of the day. And this gave him an idea. He decided he could start something like this in Sheffield. And so, the seed was sown.

Dad's success was launched by his ability to get great bands and solo singers to play in his club. But it was one particular band that really got him going and got his name known in Sheffield. He'd been booking local bands and been doing ok, but not as well as he'd liked. He heard there was a new group really making waves and so rang the band's manager, one Brian Epstein, and eventually agreed, at great expense, the services of The Beatles for £65, huge money in 1963.

Once he advertised that they were coming to Sheffield to play at his club the town went nuts, and bookings for tickets went through the roof! So much so he had to change the venue as his converted house on Pittsmore Road wasn't going to do. He had to hire the local dancehall called the Azena Ballroom.

On the 12th of February 1963, the Beatles played to a packed house, and cemented the reputation of Peter Stringfellow as a guy who could bring you the best venue for gigs and the best bands. His notoriety grew... fast.

 And over the next few years, he got many great bands and future stars that everyone has heard of. After the Beatles, the names kept coming. Pink Floyd, The Rolling Stones, The Yardbirds with Eric Clapton, Rod Stewart while he was with The Small Faces, Ike & Tina Turner, Wilson Pickett, Sonny Boy Williamson and Stevie Wonder to name but a few. Apparently, Rod Stewart bounced me on his knee when his band came to do their soundcheck. Obviously, I was very little and verging on being a toddler at the time, so I don't remember it.

It was while we still lived in Sheffield that I became more aware about what dad did and that he worked nights in a club. I just thought it was normal he was never around in the mornings. I have memories of Cockayne Place where we lived after the Mojo was closed and he opened another club called "Down Broadway'. Now I'm aware we didn't stay there for long as things were about to change.

3

LEEDS (FULL SPEED AHEAD, WITH A STOP OFF IN WAKEFIELD)

Dad always was one for not letting the grass grow under his feet. He always had his ambitions firmly on the horizon to chase, he wanted to be rich and famous, and Sheffield wasn't going to do that for him. Despite his successes with his club, he wanted a new patch and possibly a bigger venue.

He had a chance to take on a new building being developed in Leeds, the northern town further up the country above Sheffield. It was a large building, long and flat that had two floors. The ground floor was offices, I think. But the first floor was to be where dad was building his club, or more accurately "clubs" plural. As the clubs were developing only one would be opened first, while the other was still being kitted out.

It was 1970 and this was eventually going to be the first club that would be Europe's only twin nightspot or as dad also dubbed it, the "LEEDS SUPERSCENE" in large letters on the front of the clubs along with their names: "Cinderella's & Rockerfella's".

While this was going on, mum and dad were house searching.... and didn't quite find what they wanted straight away. We ended up living in Horbury, Wakefield for about a year, but it's a place I'll always remember, as this was when I started infant school. We lived in a very modern, for 1970, bungalow. We had a cat that immediately had kittens, I played outside most of the time, and we had a swinging basket chair in the lounge.

As one club opened, Rockerfella's, dad was back on the full-time nightlife and his commute was a long one. But on the Saturday nights there was a major change for me. Mum was going out to the club at night with dad now, and on the first night she left me with a very nice babysitter. I screamed the place down by all accounts. And mum was virtually climbing out of the car, but dad with great reasoning said I'd got to learn that this is how it was going to be, and I would soon calm once I realised, she wasn't going away forever.

It took a couple of weekends, but he was right.

Again, dad wasn't around much, but I do have memories of both mum and dad coming with me to the infant school very close to our house to drop me off. Another time dad came back from being at the club office during the day and as he brought his car in, I saw that his rear window had been smashed in. To this day, I don't remember what that was all about.

We had a cherry blossom tree in our back garden and my dad loved it. I think this was probably the first time I noticed that dad had other interests besides going away at night to work.

The time we had in Wakefield flew by, but I enjoyed it. The next house was far bigger and on the main ring road outside Leeds in an area called Seacroft. And it was at the top of a hill with one and a half acres of land attached, and a bus stop right outside our driveway, which ascended to the house.

Things were changing in dad's clubs too. He still put bands on, and usually two at the same time, as both sides of the club were running now, but also comedy acts, magicians and even strippers in the Cinderella's side. But both clubs were primarily dancing, drink and dining clubs. Both had 2 bars, and both had restaurants. This was a massive step up for dad, and a large leap in sophistication. Both clubs were an instant success. And for the next seven years we were THE venue to be seen at.

I was now firmly in no doubt that my dad was a night club owner, and the showmanship that dad had was already rubbing off on me, as a cheeky 6-year-old I had developed a liking for telling jokes and doing impressions of the personalities of the time. Dad took me to the club one night, and from the DJ box dressed in my suit and dickie bow I told jokes and did those impressions to all my dad's customers in the club.

I think it was in the Cinderella's side if my memory is correct. I probably went down ok with the club full of half pissed people. I don't remember if I was heckled at all, or maybe I just blocked that out of my mind, who knows?

As dad was still booking bands, the 70s were great for some big names of the day just as they were about to get gigs at larger venues as their fame grew. He had the likes of Mud and Slade just before they hit it big, and also many solo singers.

My dad got to know quite a few of the big names as his clubs were seen as a good place to break into being known, and cabarets were still in demand back then. He had one guy who dad used to book in Sheffield a fair bit called Shane Fenton. He mainly did Buddy Holly numbers and some of his own stuff. He was due to play at Rockerfella's, but he called my dad and told him he couldn't make it as his manager had double booked him and couldn't let the other guy down. But he'd be in touch soon.

Dad got on the phone and spoke to Shane's manager to see who else he had, who then told dad about a new act. He was a bit more expensive but worth it as the guy was going to knock the socks off the music world and go straight to number one.

Dad had heard this before but went for it anyway. And so, Alvin Stardust was booked. But when Alvin turned up, it was Shane. Dad went mad. "Shane what are you doing? Why didn't you tell me?"

Shane/Alvin apologised and told dad "I'm sorry Pete, but it was a big secret, I had to make a break from my old image to the new one. My manager said I couldn't tell anyone".

Dad forgave him, but the manager was right, Alvin became a very big name in the 70's with his first song in his new guise: a black leather one-piece get up with tassels hanging off the arms. This became a number 1 hit "My Coo-Ca-Choo". Many more hits followed. On a few occasions Alvin visited my mum and dad at our home. I have a great picture of Alvin, my sister and I posing with him in his classic pose. I've got his huge black finger ring on my hand... with two fingers through it. I had tiny fingers.

One-time Alvin dropped by, and for whatever reason he was on the phone in our house. By this time, I was getting pretty relaxed that Alvin was one of my dad's friends. Quite by chance one of my friends dropped by to return a couple of singles I had lent him to record.

Sure enough, he saw Alvin Stardust waltzing about on the phone in our kitchen: and since there were no mobiles in those days, so he couldn't go far. It had a cord, but the phone was screwed to the wall. My friend's mouth dropped open!

I never really spoke much to my friends about who my dad knew or who I had met... I was only about 9 or 10. I wasn't star struck except for the first time I met Alvin, but I got over it. However, my friend was right at the same point I was when I first got close to him. And like an idiot, I got a little cocky and I kind of told my friend to tell his friends too, which he did... and a few more besides.

Around the perimeter fence of our large back garden, which backed onto the local farmer's land, but was also a wooded area, the fence line was lined with a hoard of teenagers and kids all chanting "WE WANT ALVIN, WE WANT ALVIN, WE WANT ALVIN".

Like the good chap he was, he went out signed autographs and had pictures with his fans.

I believe I got into a degree of trouble with dad over that one.

But I loved living in Leeds, and Dad used to feel that I treated the place like it was my real home rather than a Sheffield boy. He was right to a degree, as this was where my childhood was formed, where I made a lot of friends, and had a few girlfriends too.

While in Leeds I also developed a knack for getting ill, and into scrapes, which probably all got kicked off with the nail in the head incident. From an early age I had already been battling asthmatic-bronchitis and other ailments along for the ride too which also included the usual stuff you can get as a kid. One time I was with my mum and dad as we went into town, so dad could buy some records for the club, and mum do a bit of shopping.

After they got what they wanted we headed over to the clubs, so dad could play some of his new records to get a real feel for them; meanwhile I was pratting around on the dance floors, one raised as a stage area, and the dancefloors around it, something he would repeat at the Hippodrome a million years later. But at this time, dad was playing his songs, and mum just sat nearby reading Cosmopolitan or whatever.

Quite out of the blue I took a bad step off the stage area and landed on the hard-wooden dancefloor chin first. There was

a moment of silence from me, and then the pain came....
then there wasn't silence from me, and yet again blood was
involved... which is what probably made it worse.

Mum and Dad sprang into action, and I was bundled into
dad's car on mum's lap. He had an E-type Jaguar at the time,
and I do remember dad was driving quickly to the nearest
hospital, which was Leeds General. There followed the obvious stitches to be done, and for some reason, I still remember
I had to have 9 in my chin. The scar for that lasted for quite a
while if I remember rightly.

During our time in Leeds Dad had really upped his position
in life, and was starting to reap the benefits of success, like
better holidays. In the beginning of moving to Leeds it was
trips to the seaside in Bridlington or Great Yarmouth, and
then my sister Karen and I were sometimes packed off with
Nannan & Grandpa Stringfellow to the coast staying in a
caravan or chalets.

But as dad's clubs became packed every night, we started going to places like Tenerife, Tunisia, Mallorca and Corfu. And
it was great, but it was on our trip to Mallorca, I think it was
that I caused my mum and dad some strife. We had a babysitter or house sitter as Karen and I preferred called Nancy, and
she came on holiday with us, supposedly so my mum and dad
could go out and have adult time together in the evenings,
safe in the knowledge that we were being cared for.

Karen and I remember this particular holiday mainly because
our dad had to give me a smack on my backside for something, I did.... well, said!

For some reason I had called her a very bad word. And on
their return Karen dutifully dobbed me in. "Daddy, Scott
called Nancy a bastard!" I can still remember the look on his
face. I loved my mum and dad and didn't like upsetting them,
but clearly, I had crossed a line.

Dad turned me over his knee and said those words that have such an effect but yet are not quite true... "This is going to hurt me more than it's going to hurt you!" Afterwards, I was sent to my bed and nothing more was spoken about it, apart from me apologising to Nancy of course. And I still don't remember to this day why I had called her a bastard!

Back at home in Leeds we had a great house with a lot of land and quite a lot of trees. In fact, the house was originally called "The Trees" but dad decided at some point that there were too many and got tree surgeons in to cut a lot of them down.

Now I didn't know much about land ownership then, and probably not a great deal more now, but I reckon dad was being very cheeky and removed some of the trees without any planning permission or informing the council before building the outside dog kennel for our two huge Great Danes dad got for us. In fact, we lived next to farmland, and it had horses and cows on it. I didn't think the farmer was into crops except for the large strip of land right behind our house and more trees off to the right behind us. I seem to remember there was some kind of feud with the farmer and my dad. I never got to find out, but it might have been something to do with the gate dad had put in that led straight onto the guy's land.

Well, that or the fact that once or twice my dad and his brother Geoff made a small kart track in the field behind and we raced our grass karts on there a few times. More about the karts later, but we tore the land up a bit. Which is probably why on one occasion I woke up one morning to look out my bedroom window to see about ten cows roaming around in our garden and eating the roses. Dad had to go chase them out.

Another time we had horses galloping around in our garden too, and they were harder to get out. So maybe the easy access gate in our fence wasn't such a good idea after all. I think at some point the gate was removed and the fence back to being just that. Oh, and also it had to have a couple more fence layers put on to make it higher, not to keep the horses out, it was done to keep our huge Great Danes in!

So much happened while in Leeds, and not all of it was good, but the good things in life seemed to happen most of the time. Dad was also getting very wealthy at the time, too, I guess and wanted to make sure we, Karen and I, didn't want for anything... but we were spoiled rotten, I think.

Not every kid had a motorbike and a grass kart in their back gardens. But we did. And Dad, together with his brother Geoff, got me and my cousins a kart each. We would go, for a while, to a small track behind a pub out the other side of Seacroft not far from us. It was like having out own private test track.

I'm guessing my dad knew the owner... but also knowing dad, he just saw it one day and decided we would take the karts there. It was like dad could do anything. His personality was developing, and his can-do attitude was well in place. But he still found time to relax. In the summer of 1976 it was, at the time, the hottest summer on record, and the whole country was melting.

Barbeques were everywhere. My dad organised one in our garden, lots of friends and some of his staff from the club came too. It was a lovely hot Sunday. At the time Karen and I also had had off-road motorbikes which we used to belt around the garden on. Our cousins had them too. We were all very, very spoiled when I look back on it all now. But mum and dad made it a rule of the barbie day to not get the bikes out. We were fine about it, as it was raging hot and we always wore our helmets, boots, gloves and suits. It was way too warm for that.

The barbeque was going well, everyone in swimming gear and very much enjoying themselves. Drink was probably also involved... it was the 70s after all. Out of the blue dad decided that the motorbikes could come out... to keep the kids happy, apparently.

Off went I to go get my kit on. Pretty soon I was belting around the garden on my self-made track. But then dad decided he wanted a play, not only that, he also wanted to take one of his friends for a ride on my sister's bike, the Honda XR75, which was a great scramble bike. He jumped on with only his swimming trunks on and no helmet, as did his friend. The bike had good springs on it, but with two up it was a bit bouncy. I followed behind as a dad scooted off on my course. There was one bit that had a jump between two trees, not a high jump, but as dad aimed for it, his stupid friend on the back got a little freaked, which probably only served to egg my dad on. Just as he was deciding to not go over it, he changed his mind went for it and at that moment the twit on the back jumped off. This unsettled the bike as it hit the small hump which served as my makeshift jump. As dad went through and over, the bike jumped up with the rear as the springs were set free for the passenger's arse. Dad was pitched up forward on the front wheel, and as the bike tipped over to one side, he lost balance and the bike came down on my dad's left leg.

He managed to move the bike off as some people watching who were laughing then realised, he wasn't kidding around by still being on the floor. He told us later that he noticed his leg pointing at a slightly alarming angle, and he himself manoeuvred his leg back into position. It became apparent it wasn't good, and an ambulance was called.

Dad spent some time in hospital. I forget which one. He had torn ligaments in his left knee, but he was on morphine which had quite an effect on him. While laid up he started writing stories, poems and even songs which included an idea for a full orchestra. He even taped it on a cassette player. Meanwhile, my mum went into work during the day and did some things for him that she could do. And as mum was the poet and secret songwriter of the family, it was a time of role-reversal, which was interesting.

Eventually, he was let out of the hospital but was not able to go upstairs at home. So, we rigged up the sun lounger from the shed where it lived ready to be brought out on sunny days. We set it up in the lounge, with a small table beside him and there he lived for a while, with his leg encased in plaster. Now there was only so long you can keep dad in one place for, and since he was off the heavy medication, he got restless, and really wanted to go back to work.

One day, while Karen and I were somewhere else, and my mum had gone out, dad hatched a plan. He had a Rolls-Royce Silver shadow at the time, and it was an automatic with the gear changer on the steering column. and a virtual bench seat across the front. He, with the aid of a walking stick, got out into his car and managed to get in put his leg up, complete with plaster cast, on the passenger side and drove off into Leeds. When my mum came back, she saw the car was gone, dashed in the house to see if dad was ok, thinking the car had been stolen, only to find dad was gone too. She had no idea where he had gone, and as there were no such thing as mobile phones back then, she was at a loss of what to do. When he returned, she went nuts at him.

Over time the plaster cast came off, and he kept up walking with his walking cane, a rather nice one my mum found in an antique shop. He used it for quite a while. In fact, around this time my mum was adding sequins to his suits for nightclub work and he took to wearing hats too, well... this was the 70s and the cane added to his outfit. He was always the showman at heart.

Cars while in Leeds

A Car is generally seen as a status symbol, and dad certainly was keen to be seen in something either different or that stood out in a subtle but obvious way. Sounds like an impossibility doesn't it? But dad managed it.

While in Sheffield he quietly progressed from borrowing cars, to hiring them and then owning. The earliest one I remember was his Bentley, an old one. And in those days, they were not sophisticated but still elegant. I think he was trying to be like John Lennon or was it George Harrison? Who had the multicoloured Rolls-Royce?

But dad didn't go that far with his. Next up was his Vauxhall Viva Brabham. That car design, as the name suggests, was a marketing ploy to sell this car with sporty styling tips and supposedly fast performance was a tip of a hat towards F1 world champion, Sir Jack Brabham. It looked great with its chrome wheels and matte-black bonnet, with extra go-faster stripes on the side. However, it broke down... a lot. He had a Hillman Imp for a short while before we moved to Wakefield, and then he started trying newer cars that were popular at the time.

The white Chrysler Avenger was first, and dad came back from the club once with the rear window smashed in, as I mentioned before. Maybe someone didn't like being thrown out of the club while being too drunk? Or maybe dad had been making moves on someone's chick... Who knows?

Then he had a mild flirtation with a deep maroon Rover 3500 TC. When we got to Leeds and moved into the big house on the hill of Seacroft Ring Road and after the Rover went, dad really started to get into his cars, and my mum wasn't left out either.

Dad nearly bought a few things, but eventually got one of the greatest status symbols of the time, and possibly still is: The

Jaguar E-type V12. It, too, was Maroon in colour with a sun-roof. Our dog Winston the Great Dane loved that car. Mum used to come pick me up from school with the dog's head sticking out of the roof with his bum in one of the back seats and feet all the way to the floor of the car.

Dad once was on his way back from some other town on the motorway, when suddenly the rear hatch boot door flew off. It was enough to make him think about changing his car, which he soon did, and took possession of a Jensen Intercep-tor Mk3. It was white with a black vinyl roof. It was great, I can still hear the engine and smell the leather of that car to this day, however, that had its problems too.

Dad used to go on the odd long trip, and the Jensens had a minor problem with that, the thermostat used to blow a fuse and without the fan the coolant would get way too hot. So that had to go after we did an impromptu trip to London to pick it up. We went hiring a car with all of us in on the trip for a weekend break.

Dad tried to stay buying British and followed the Jensen up with his first Rolls-Royce, the Silver shadow which he had in a champagne gold colour was really nice and fitted his ambitions very well. At the same time his business partner and brother Geoff had a Silver shadow too, only his was in a silver-grey colour. If I'd been aware of such things at such a young age, I'd think my dad and his brother were being like the Krays of the north.

My mother's cars were pretty iconic too, though we didn't know it then. She went from a beige Mini 1000 to an Orange MG Midget pretty quickly and finished up with a Metallic green Vauxhall Chevette GL. In which I learnt how to change gear in on my way back from school from the passenger seat of course.

Car wise things were about to get a lot more interesting once we moved to a new house again.

* * *

Meanwhile, back in Leeds in the social world, Dad was very busy and Cinderella's & Rockerfella's was doing really well. He did more than just put on cabaret shows and have up and coming bands, singers and comedy acts. He also got into the fashion show venue business, and the Miss world type pageants too. He just got on with doing what he did best, created a good night out for as many people as he could cram into his clubs. But he was getting itchy feet and thinking about pastures new for a new challenge. We spent seven years in Leeds and my relationship with dad was great. I may never have seen him for breakfast before I went to school, but we got on great.

The night life he had never really struck me as a problem. It was normal life. But dad worked hard at all of it. Sometimes we had disagreements, but a lot of the time it was great. We even developed a kind of routine by liking some of the same TV shows and watching them together. "Star Trek" was the main memory for me. But also "Fawlty Towers" and "Monty Python's Flying Circus" and "Columbo" too. However, virtually every night, dad would go get changed for work, and off he went. He worked every night, no nights off, well rarely... but it was his show, and he ran it.

Our fallouts were very few, and sometimes quite funny, like the time I found a pack of very saucy playing cards hidden in the house. Well not hidden, more stupidly left out for a sharp-eyed nine-year-old to spot. Who then took outside to show his friends, where much giggling was had and gasps of disbelief at what these grown-ups on the cards were doing.

Suddenly there was a sharp clip round the ear from dad who had strolled up behind me and took the cards off me without a word being said. It was never brought up, except by my mum to me who thought it was all very funny.

But Leeds was losing its spark for dad, or he just wanted something new. And so, he started scouting around at other towns... and just over the hill was Lancashire and the slightly bigger City of Manchester. His ambitions rose.

4

WHO WANTS TO BE A MILLIONAIRE? (DAD DOES!)

The move to Manchester was a big step. As the song goes, "Who wants to be a millionaire?" Well, Dad certainly did, so he sold the twin night spot in Leeds to the entertainment leisure group MECCA. As dad had found an interesting premises in the heart of Manchester in West Mosley Street. It was a large single room underground plot, with an entrance that looked like a twenty by twenty ornate box, but through the double doors was a staircase leading down. Talk about contrast, dad went from a first-floor double club, to an enormous underground studio, which he named "The Millionaire Club".

Meanwhile back in the domestic side, Karen and I had to stay with some people in a house near our new school for a short while until contracts were exchanged on our new house in Cheadle Hulme.

This was 1977, Star Wars was going to hit the silver screen, and disco music was very big thanks in part to the film Saturday Night Fever with the Bee Gees and Michael Jackson. Both were about to take the world by storm. Abba was still going strong and Meatloaf was about set up residence in the top 40 for the next seven years with their album "Bat out of Hell."

On top of that, punk rock was gaining strength and upsetting a lot of people. However, a lot of the singers and bands that dad hosted over the years were becoming very big too, Rod Stewart and Fleetwood Mac to name a couple.

But dad was making large waves as well. The club was one of chic opulence, with a décor of brown and cream, contrasted with chrome railings and the latest disco lighting. At the entrance as one went down the staircase dad had put a real Rolls-Royce front grill complete with flying lady (aka: Spirit of Ecstasy) on the wall above. As one descended into the club, you really were being given the feeling of being somewhere exclusive.

Dad wasn't booking acts so much now as the demand for just dancing to disco music took over that side, and really the club wasn't properly set up for it. Having said that he still did some interesting shows, like fashion shows with themes, and Halloween shows, fancy dress doos around Christmas. And we always were a great venue for Christmas Eve and New Year's Eve.

When we settled into our new house, which was directly behind my new school, mum and dad started doing what they did at the last house, which is to, make changes within. They did it in Leeds too, got the house how they wanted it, then moved. There was loads to do in this large detached house, lots of wood to strip back, and a spot of kitchen and bathroom remodelling.

Karen started at the main school behind our house, and I started in the junior school a few streets away, which was still a part of the school behind our house. It was called Hulme Hall School. It was a big change for me personally. This was the first time I was aware of having to start again in meeting new kids and making new friends. Again, dad didn't feature in the mornings, but it was a short walk to school and an even shorter one to the big school behind us. It didn't take too long to settle in, and dad bought himself one of the new sound cine cameras, so any parent invited events at the school were documented by my wild dad.

It was here I got to know a few kids who even to this day are close friends of mine, and some who I met up with through Facebook and organised reunions ... and that's a lot of years ago now.

The Big Holiday

Dad was really getting into his stride at this time, and this was a time of growth in every way. Our holidays got more interesting too, in 1978 we went to America. I had wanted to go there ever since the early 70's through watching the American cop TV show Starsky & Hutch. And here we were about to jet off to California on a jumbo jet, which was another dream come true.

Dad being dad, we did it on a grander scale, we were going to do what became known as the "Golden Triangle". Which meant we were going to Los Angeles, San Francisco and Las Vegas. And after we landed, we would hire a big American car and take a road trip. Looking back now I'm so glad dad took his precious sound cine camera with us. He filmed virtually… everything, but a lot of it was a bit fast and blurry. A lot of it was great.

We did the Universal studios tour, Disneyland, and spent time with his good friend Buddy Greco, who was one of those American crooning singing stars. The guy had a great house and swimming pool. I think Dad was very taken with his lifestyle.

Onto San Francisco and views of the rolling hills of city street just like the ones in saw in another cop show back home. And a trip in a helicopter over the famous Golden Gate bridge. I don't remember much about this part of the trip other than the streets, cable cars and the amount of flared trousers, even on the police officers who also wore guns!

We found a street vendor who made customised t-shirts and have whatever you wanted on them. Dad being dad just had this guy making a load of t-shirts for us, and some special proper over-the-top shiny jackets with lettering of "The Millionaire Club" emblazoned all over them. My mum and I still have them!

However, one night Karen and I were left at the hotel as Dad was itching to get a look of Frisco night life, and then to meet friends and generally buzz around the club scene... even on holiday the work-life he chose was never far away, except this time he was getting ideas and getting very into it all well... all but the near constant turning down the offers of drugs! I found out many years later that on that holiday what he saw was a huge influence on what was yet to come.

On to Las Vegas and with the camera out the roof of the hire car, we got a treat of the night lights of the Vegas strip, a mass of blurry images. Dad was very struck by Vegas for obvious reasons. The whole place was nightlife heaven, or hell, depending on how you looked at it. We were staying in an apartment that was in the same block as my mum and dads' friends Fred & Marylin Kassler who were, to my eyes then an old couple, but more likely around the age I am now... 50s.

They were like something out of the Flintstones, both had obviously been married a long time, and were very comfortable with having a go at each other in front of others. This was not offensive, more like a likeable double act. It was so hot out in Vegas, something like 110 degrees plus. Karen and I spent a lot of time in the pool and dad would join in the fun in the pool too.

At night the lights on all the hotels were amazing. These days it's a lot bigger and brighter, if that were possible. But back then it was still amazing to us. And Dad's camera work took on a new type of freaky, I think the battery was running low or something, but there was a lot of very quick panning of blurred lights and iconic signs as he waved the cine camera out of the car window while driving, but also the sound was like we were all doped up on something and we all sounded a few octaves lower. Dad sounded like deep opera singer and mum like a bloke, it was really funny to see when played back.

Again, mum and dad wanted to get into the night scene, but as casinos didn't allow children, it was an unusual arrangement that we came to, to solve this one. They were asked to meet up with some people in a hotel called "Circus, Circus" which was unique in looking like a huge big top circus tent. They had had a ground floor which was the size of a couple of football fields, and on an open first floor above in a giant circle was also fairground type games for kids to explore, generally with their parents.

Above that, there was a trapeze suspended from the huge ceiling. It was a spectacular sight, and one I had seen before on the James Bond film "Diamonds are Forever" which featured a lot of Las Vegas, including this casino/hotel/funhouse.

Dad told Karen and I to float around the fairground bit for about an hour, and we would meet up at a specified location when that hour was up. Not the kind of thing that would be thought about today, but dad was always thinking of ways round a problem, that's the kind of guy he was.

Sure enough, after we had spent all the quarters and dollars that he plied us with to spend on the amusements, we went to the meeting place, they were late, and just when I was starting to get worried... Mum and dad homed into view, in that order as my mum was the first to slightly panic, with dad in her wake, clearly not so worried.

However, the next night of them going out on the town, a better arrangement was reached, we were left in the company of Marylin at their apartment and left to watch one of the hundreds of channels on the TV. I think Fred went with them. We were happy, and mum and dad had a more relaxing night out visiting more iconic casinos. Again, Vegas was working its magic on dad and giving him lots to think about.

We were soon back to LA and at the airport, ready to go home. Strange how the big adventure seemed to come and go so fast. America made a big impression on all of us, more so on dad.

Holidays with dad always felt magical, he was the undisputed leader of fun. Sure, he could relax in the sun, sunbathing, and reading with a dip in the pool to cool down. But he wouldn't be like this every day. he'd get restless and we'd soon be off somewhere in search of something interesting.

Back to Manchester it was, and home to Cheadle Hulme. But the summer wasn't quite over, and dad was not only back into the swing of work, but the weekends became a time of private parties at home. There are two particular parties that stick in my mind, both of which Karen and I were not involved with, as these were adult dinner parties. On one occasion, I was in my bed trying to get to sleep, even though Karen and I had sat at the top of the stairs listening to the noisy adult banter for a good hour or so, when I heard someone shout ,"Oh my god Peter and ? (can't remember her name now) is outside playing tennis naked!"

I jumped out of bed and looked out of my window to see the back-garden flood light on and my dad playing softball tennis with some woman who was also naked. They were batting the ball to each other. It never occurred to me what my mum might think about it, only that it was one of my dad's mad spontaneous moments... which it most probably was, and more than likely alcohol fuelled.

Another time, after we had gone back to school, the weekends were still party time, and more so on a Sunday night as the club wasn't open on Sundays. Being the night owl, I'm sure Dad had these parties because he knew he couldn't sleep and was restless. However come one Monday morning I got up for School, I think by this time Karen was at Collage, I got dressed, had breakfast and was about to leave for school, when I thought it was polite to go knock on the lounge door where the party was still going on. I knocked, and then a bit louder as there was still some music going on and chit-chat... there was a bit of Shushing going on and the music was lowered.... "Who is it?" shouts dad.

"It's me, Scott!" I say. A short-hushed conversation followed, and dad shouts back, "Go to bed!"

Well, that was confusing, I stood there with my coat on and my school bag. I shouted back "I'm going to school!"

This time I could hear some of the words. I'm pretty sure there was more than mum and dad in there as I could hear another voice. And Dad asking, "What time is it?"

The other voice said "Oh shit, Pete, its half past eight..."

Dad again... "Er, ok Scotty. See ya later"

And that was more or less it! I toddled off to school, again not fazed by any of it.... Obviously, years later I wanted to know what was going on, but decided it wasn't a problem, and hey it's a good story. Dad was just not Mr. Normal... whatever that was?

Cars While in Manchester

Dad had really come on in life, the house in Cheadle Hulme was lovely, and one I would love to own now myself. It had a long driveway and two garages that could fit two cars in one and one in the other. And this really was the age of dad having some wonderful cars.

He arrived in Cheshire, which was arguably the right car to be seen in, driving the Gold Rolls-Royce Silver Shadow. But in 1978 he got to know some really nice guys who owned a great car showroom only a few streets away from the club called "Bauer & Millett" and he saw something in there that got his car pulse racing. He part exchanged his Rolls for a 1977 Chevrolet Corvette Stingray in chocolate-metallic brown.

Now that sounds like a terrible colour for a car, but honestly it looked great, and at the age of 12 I got to drive it at an old disused airfield where other people used to go and fly remote-controlled airplanes and helicopters. And a few other cars were flashing about, too. However, dad put me on two cushions on the driver's side, and away I went learning to drive a very flash first car to drive with a V8 engine and an automatic gearbox to make it easier.

Not long after he swapped mum's car from the Chevette GL for a lovely coral coloured Alfa Romeo Alfasud Sprint. And then he really got carried away. I think his accountant must have told him to invest in nice cars for future reference. He decided to get another car, a Jeep CJ7 Golden Eagle which was white with gold lettering on, and gold-coloured wheels, and it was very high off the ground.

I loved it even though it had no power steering for whatever reason, I got to drive that one too. This is still a car I wish to own to this day myself. But he didn't stop there! The Stingray went, and a huge Cadillac Eldorado Convertible took its place, even though the Jeep stayed for a while too. The Cadillac, he later confessed to me, was his favourite car that he ever owned. And it makes sense, because it matched his ego. Bright, showy and everyone noticed it. Soon he decided to let go of the Jeep, which was a bugger, but he wanted me to go with him on a trip to look at cars....

I was 15 years old and very happy to go with him for that. We went to a couple of nice garages, one in Wilmslow, the extremely posh village not far from Cheadle and where most of the Manchester United players and the well to do people live these days.

Stratton's is still a very exclusive garage today, but in 1980 they were still growing, and my dad wanted to drive the Aston Martin Vantage, which was a lovely metallic blue convertible, with cream interior. He was quite taken with it after a test drive. In all honesty it suited him down to the ground. But we visited another garage later in the day, again owned by someone who he had met in his club. Sackville Garage was on the way into Manchester, and in the centre of the showroom was my dream car, A Porsche Turbo 3.3. It was in the colour that was called in Porsche circles, Guards Red.

It wasn't a deep maroon like dads old E-Type, nor was it a Ferrari red. But for me it was love at first sight. Strangely enough, I don't remember us taking it out for a test, but we must have. I was sold on it, which was a shame as I wasn't in control of the chequebook.

On our drive home dad said, "Well Scotty, what do you think?"

I went straight to the point, as I was still thinking about it… "I think you should get the Porsche!… it's perfect."

But dad shook his head, "I don't know, that convertible Aston was really nice, and it was an automatic, which is perfect for me."

He wasn't wrong there, gears for dad were for other people, whenever he changed gear, he always looked unsure or just uncomfortable doing it. He was even worse in a left-hand drive car. If you've ever watched someone try to play tennis with their other hand… it was a bit like that!

Dad decided to have a think about it all. I couldn't get what was to think about. "Dad the Aston is £40,000 and the Porsche is only £26,500.... You could be saving.... er..." my maths wasn't great, but I worked it out "£13,500".

He just looked across at me and grinned! Now my dad could play poker, and he was really good at it, so the grin was nothing to go by... it could mean anything.

About a week later, I was back in Sheffield staying with my grandparents for the weekend, and dad came to pick me up. This was a surprise as it was normally my mum. I went to the door with my Nannan, and was really pleased to see him, and as my grandparents were in a cul-de-sac, but without a drive, you could see all the cars parked out front. And amongst the Mr. average cars was the beautiful guards red Porsche Turbo...

I went bonkers... "YOU GOT IT, YOU GOT IT, YOU GOT IT!" dad was stopping me from going outside and teasing me.

"Yes, I got that Fiat instead, isn't it nice?" he said while pointing at the car next to the obvious as the nose on your face lovely red Porsche.... But he gave in, and I was off with my overnight bag blazing a trail to the car. I can't remember if I said bye to my Nannan and grandpa I was that excited, but I do remember they were smiling as I went.

Dad was great at teasing, but the Porsche was the only car that ever frightened him. On our way back to Cheadle Hulme that evening we got on the snake pass... this is a wonderful twisting country road that was fantastic when a sunny day was had, but treacherous when the weather was bad.

Thankfully it was a nice drive back, and Dad did put his foot down somewhat, which I loved. But you could see the knuckles on his hands on the steering wheel pure white as he gripped it with his eyes looking like they were on stalks and afraid to blink. He reckons that night he got 150 mph, but since all my experience from my racing, I'm pretty sure it was more like 130, which is still going some. We could feel the front of the car wanting to lift up with the speed. Again, many years later, I would know how to cure that, I just wish I knew it then.

I loved that car, and when the time came for dad to sell it, I didn't speak to him for two whole weeks afterwards. But I did get to hear dad say the F-word for the first time while we had it. He had to take me to the dentist during the day. While getting the car out of the garage and turning it round in our driveway, he ran over a nail... as I stood outside the car at the time, I saw and heard the tire pop.

Dad opened his car door slightly and looked at the rear right flat tire. "Oh, Fuck!' He said out loud. And then, as was his way, he'd look at me and say, "Sorry Scotty!" He always apologised after swearing. That magically stopped after I turned 18 some years later.

Almost all at once Dad sold all the cars. Porsche, Jeep and the Cadillac all went. And in their place came a brand-new BMW 318i. This was when the club in London was coming to life, and dad was doing lots of trips down south, so the thirsty ones had to go. It was while dad had this car that it got written off, and it wasn't even him that did it. He lent his car to a newspaper gossip columnist friend of his from London. He came up north on the train and then borrowed dad's car to go to Derby to see something at an antique shop. But on the twisty country roads, the guy got too confident with his driving and promptly rolled the car and put himself in hospital.

This was bad news. The guy was alright, just a cut head and concussion. But dad hadn't insured the guy, and the guy hadn't insured himself. So, dad had to lash out to get another car, and this time he got a Mercedes Benz 350SL. This turned out to be the one car he kept the longest. And even when he got rid of it, it was passed on to my mother when he decided to get a new one. But by that time, we were in London.

Goodbye Manchester

Dad was getting restless again, and since the America trips his ideas were getting far more ambitious. He went looking at properties in Birmingham, London and San Francisco. Yep, he was really seriously looking at moving us lock, stock, and barrel to the USA.

 I think he was looking at all three because whatever happened, in his mind we were on our way to pastures new. Birmingham was the strange one for me, but maybe a small jump to a fairly local city that was on the way to London or elsewhere was just so he could develop somewhere that was just a steppingstone before his next move. He was always thinking bigger or, like that game of Risk, just thinking about strategy to get to his ultimate goal of world club domination perhaps?

We were so close to jumping over the pond, that his brother Geoff told his wife of the plan, even though dad wasn't at the point of no return. And of course, Karen and I had no clue of any of this.

Just when he was dashing back and forth to America with visions of making it big in the US, he got a phone call from his solicitor about some premises he had looked into in London. And unbeknownst to us, he had gone quite far down the road of committing to a property in the big city... he'd even got as far as seeking planning permission to do building work on a plot in Covent Garden.

The solicitor was saying that he had been granted the permission to go ahead. The brakes came on for Frisco, which I think my dad was a little sad about himself, as he had been seduced by the Californian garden of love and peace. But this was a shot in the arm, and reality that whichever direction he was going, it was going to be different.

So, it was going to be all change again, and as I understand from finding out later, all those that were in on the America plan were not happy. But you sometimes have to make hard decisions if the alternative is going to keep you going.

Now Manchester wasn't doing badly, quite the reverse, and so dad found a buyer for the Millionaire, and with that money plus a substantial loan, he went full steam ahead with the new club.

Our time up north was coming to an end, and my school days in Cheadle Hulme were being interspersed with something I had an interest in, drama classes, and so my mum and dad found the guy who ran the Manchester Youth Theatre. And as dad was building His new club in London, I auditioned and got into theatre life for the first time. I was always of a mind that when life after school arrived, I'd be a DJ like my dad. So, getting on stage was also good training for potential showmanship in my future club life that was yet to come.

August the 1st 1980 was the date that the flagship of my dad's achievements opened.

STRINGFELLOWS in London was born.

Dad did a lot of commuting during this time, and he ended up getting a small house in Islington in north London. It was a place I would get to know when we all moved down.

During this time of change, I was discovering acting, which was great to be in the company of like-minded people. Drama classes at regular school was always bittersweet. On the one hand, you got to get your creative side going and improvise scenes, which I loved, but the downside was half of the class weren't interested and disrupting the thing I and some others actually wanted to learn.

I got to really dislike certain kids at Hulme Hall School. Because they just showed off, tore everyone else down by being complete idiots. But at the Manchester Youth theatre I discovered a different way, when everyone in the room is keen and want to work together it became a lot more fun. And pretty soon I was in the play "Oh What a Lovely War" at the Wythenshawe Theatre. Just a couple of small parts and three very small lines which I still remember to this day. This, in turn, gave may parents an idea. I was to audition for a stage school in London, which sounded both great and daunting at the same time to me.

But before any of that went further, there was something else to think about: Now my family were very into following trends of the day, from roller skating to fashion. Me not so much, but they had all got their hair permed, Mum, Dad and Karen. It was like living with the Jacksons, and I was next on the hit list. I wouldn't do it because I wasn't wanting to look like a Michael Jackson wannabe, but more importantly, I didn't want to get the piss taken out of me at school.

But they were relentless, and in the end, I agreed to have it done, but not until I'd left Hulme Hall School. I didn't want the school bullies having a fun time at my expense, or my friends giving me gip either. So right after the summer theatre play, I went for it, even though I knew that as it was going to grow out, I'd probably end up looking like a girl.

After I had it done, we were off down south. And since I'd managed to pass the audition to get into the Arts Educational Stage School, I was turning up to meet new people that had no idea I'd had anything else but curly hair.

Mission accomplished!

5

DOWN SOUTH (LONDON LIFE)

I don't exactly remember the day we moved to London. But I do know it was a massive change from what I was used to. As it was in the case of Cheadle Hulme, we weren't moving into our actual home, we were to live in the cottage that dad and close friend and, at the time, general manager Roger, had rented to live in for a while.

Roger had got himself a house since then, and we were going to be here for a few months. This was 1981. I had already stayed at this house when I came to London for my audition for the school that I would go to... well it was a cottage, and it was a strange place. It was white with ivy climbing all over the front. Sounds nice doesn't it?

It was... but it was down an alley that had a large faded and weather-beaten green gate at the top of a very narrow driveway sort of place which backed onto the main road of Islington High street. I still remember some of the address. 26a Islington High Street. And the gate had a small Judas door in one side, but more curious was the faded sign over the top... it said, "The Blue Kettle Café" and the cottage at the bottom was to be our home.

It had a real homemade feel about it, and it was small, but had two flights of stairs. How it was ever a café, I'll never know. Dad used to park his Mercedes 350SL outside the green gates right on the busy high street. But one night he came out to find the car had been vandalised, by kids or a disgruntled customer. Who knows? For all I knew it might have been a very pissed off boyfriend of some woman that my dad had seduced. (obviously I wouldn't know that at the time, but the thought did cross my mind many years later.)

They had thrown brake fluid over the bonnet. That may not sound so bad, but brake fluid isn't meant for paint work on cars, and he had to get it sorted out at great cost. After that he'd get the car in behind the gates.

So, there we were, in one of the busiest cities in the world. I had my curly hair, and when I wasn't at school I didn't go far. I stayed in the area, went to the Kentucky Fried Chicken place a lot, sometimes down to the antique market area. There was also a real fresh fruit and veg outdoor market not far away. Dad would frighten me to death whenever he bought stuff there, as he would pull out a rolled-up wad of £20-pound notes. This was just before "Only fools and Horses" came on the TV. I swear he might have been a Del boy had he been born south of the Thames.

And where were mum and dad? Well, they both worked at the club. My mum got into doing the memberships, and PR side, which is what she did for a while at the Millionaire club before we left. Here, she got right into it. And Dad was really burning the candle at both ends to get the club noticed, and not just the club. He was beginning to be known as the club owner in his own right. This was venturing into the higher society that he'd always wanted to be a part of. To be famous, or to give it its new name: celebrity!

Right from his early days of the church hall dance clubs, dad was itching to be famous. He wanted to be a singer. But the clubs took him in that other pursuit that consumes some people. He wanted to be rich! Rich and famous would be a bonus, but one he actively got himself into. London is a hard place to get famous, and because he had the right ingredients for his club, the fame bit kind of snowballed because of the famous people he got coming in.

Looking after them and then letting the press know in the gossip columns was key to the clubs and his rise. The fact he was a bit of a showman was also a factor. You can't be up-front without the confidence and charisma of a born show-off and dad was certainly that. He also learned a few things when rubbing shoulders with the megastars. Dad was never blinded by his own light when around other celebs.

When 1982 came around a lot of things happened. We had moved into our own home, this time it was a large apartment on the Marylebone Road, which was part of one of the main road arteries into London. It was almost where the A40 finished, the almost direct route from or to Oxford.

18 Harley House was a large 12 room abode. My bedroom was at the back, with no view but a fire escape in the middle of the large complex beyond. I didn't really like living on a main road in a city that never truly slept. But my life was of commuting on the London underground system. From Baker Street station it was 5 stops to the Barbican station on either the Metropolitan or Circle lines. I would get up get myself dressed, have breakfast, sometimes with mum, never with dad, and then with every schoolbook I possessed in my bag, off I'd trot to stage school.

All the time I was at school my dad was going from strength to strength, the papers were lauding him, and Stringfellows became *the* place to be seen. It attracted the great and the good from stage and screen, a lot of famous bands or singers would come let their hair down at Strings.

My dad had a habit of coming back from work with a pile of the newspapers, so on a morning before I went to school, I would scan through a couple over my Rice Krispies. Now the thing about our press, or more accurately the tabloid press;

they like to build someone up, so they can knock them down again. So it was with us.

One morning the middle pages of one of those crappy "tomorrow's chip paper" rags had done a full double middle page on my dad, and likened us, as a family, of being something out of Dallas or Dynasty, which were the two biggest TV shows at the time. I suppose it was a sly way of complimenting and yet stirring up something about us that never existed. I can't remember what the story was exactly about now, but it was a hatchet job. And all designed to stir up a response and sell papers. But I, being a 15/16-year-old young lad, didn't have a good day at school that day. I just didn't know what would be said there. You can sometimes lose friends because of what the crappy press says.

But this was how the press treated the well-known, especially if it was a slow day in the rest of the world. And the press would make shit up, just to rattle someone's cage, as a public argument sold papers.

I grew to hate the press at that time. They never thought about the families of those they were picking on and the stories were usually overblown versions of a more innocent situation. They speculated with impunity as if it was the gospel truth, and then once the target celeb made enough noises about litigation, a decent financial pay-out was made with a public press apology printed soon after, usually buried amongst the small print. This was nothing compared to the large lettered headlines that ruined many a family's happy lives. And the trouble is, it never truly goes away. The stories can and will be reminded of in future stories good or bad.

But on occasion, my dad would do things that the press had no idea about, or not interested in at the time because they were chasing some other poor sod about their private lives.

He used to have a very 70's approach to somethings in life, like drink driving for instance. He never drank over the top, but certainly more than you should to get behind a wheel, he wasn't the greatest of drivers at the best of times. He had a lovely Rolls-Royce Corniche convertible for a while.

One night while driving back home from the club in the early hours, he was pulled over by two policemen on the street. It was a new young lad being trained for the beat with an experienced old hand. And by all accounts, the older policeman had asked the young lad to pull over a driver just to see how he did. But as my dad rounded the corner, he took the turn very wide and obviously not quite in control properly, so they pulled him over.

Now my dad got on very well with the police, and the old hand recognised dad straight away. Because he was obviously not quite sober, he was asked to do a breath test. Dad failed it. But Dad being dad knew that he could push for the option for a sample back at the station, because the bags back then were not always accurate, unlike now. He also knew it would buy him more time.

He failed that too. Apparently, the old policeman was quite apologetic to dad and said he couldn't have stopped the young lad as it would have set a bad example. He was in training after all. So, in the end he lost his driving licence for two years, I think it was. Good job his work wasn't far away, but I did get the job to drive him to work during the day. Yep I was 17 at the time, and I was working for dad rebuilding the Hippodrome inside.

And here I was driving a huge Rolls-Royce to and from the west end of London. If looks could kill, I was a dead man every trip on my way home. In the end, I couldn't do it anymore, not so much about the looks, more about the crazy drivers in London, and the fear of getting involved in even a minor shunt, let alone the real possibility of being pulled by the police myself for looking so young driving about in a Rolls-Royce.

He ended up selling the car and trying out cycling to work, he got one of those folding bikes, but also had suspension on the wheels. He wasn't sure if you could get done for drink cycling, but after getting pulled again by a bobby on the beat, he decided to go the whole hog and got a chauffeur with his own limo, which lasted for five years because he found it gave him more freedom to relax and drink without fear of jeopardising himself or anyone else on the road. Great, if you can afford that kind of thing.

6

HIPPODROME LIFE AND THE START OF RACING CARS

Dad used to go to charity events that raised money for lots of worthwhile causes. And he was very generous with his contributions. Just after celebrating the clubs first year in London in 1981. Dad became a contributor to the "Applause young variety club of Great Britain, Race Nite".

It was a fun event with an improvised race across the ballroom dance floor of the Intercontinental Hotel in London. With hobby-horses for steeds, and tables entering chosen guests as riders. It was a right laugh, but as with all these things, other than a three-course meal before the fun, there was also an auction. Which, when you think about it, is what the night was all about.

The chance to raise more money. In that auction was a generous package for some paid-for dining with champagne at Stringfellows. But there were other things, like a "Motor Racing Package" which was two grandstand tickets to the British F1 Grand Prix and two tickets for the Page & Moy tour to the Le Mans 24 hours. These along with some bound copies of Grand Prix International signed by that year's World Champion (Nelson Piquet) who was also an initial trial at Brands Hatch Racing School.

You can guess I was on the edge of my seat when that was mentioned. And Dad being the super dad he was, Bid on it.

After a short tussle with someone else on the room, my dad won it at the princely sum of £250, which even now I think was a bargain! But at the time a huge amount of money to me... and I was still only 15 at the time.

Another good story for that night was the star prize, which was a beautiful sword made by the shaving people Wilkinson's. It was a very special sword, as it had been inscribed with the date and names of HRH Prince Charles and Princess Diana to commemorate their wedding, which this was a very limited-edition piece. And my dad went on a bidding war with the well-known actress of the 80's Diane Keen, who was also a friend of my mum and dad's.

Diane won it with a bid of £2000. Which again, was a huge amount of money then. I think she shocked herself, and afterwards Dad offered to buy it off her if she woke up next morning regretting the extravagant purchase, which he ended up doing. The said sword is now with my mum on her wall at her house. And I'm sure some day it will be passed on to me too.

Back to 1982. When '82 came around dad was going from strength to strength, and those British Grand Prix grandstand tickets were going to get used. Dad elected to take me to Brands Hatch for the race, as the grandstand was the right place to be for dad. There was a little hospitality schmoozing to be done.

However, on our way there we did encounter a huge amount of traffic, stood still traffic. Eventually dad decided to park the car in a safe place off the road and we walked the rest of the way. It was a hell of a trek, but it was worth it. The seats were fantastic, right opposite the pits and easy to see one or two of my racing heroes. Dad saw a few friends of his in the grandstand. So, he got to chat while I was driver-spotting. I recognised a few people around me but couldn't quite place them. I later realised that one guy dad got chatting to was

George Harrison. I'm afraid I only had eyes for the track, so the unique moment was a little lost on me. I now wish I'd been a bit more interested in talking to George, as he was a mad F1 fan and not just there for the PR opportunity.

In time the race began, and the raw sound of the cars taking off right in front of us with the vibrations filling the air too. It was wonderful. I was engulfed in it all and loving every second. Meanwhile, quite amazingly, Dad fell asleep! I was amazed, but it was very funny. Considering the hours he put into work, I wasn't really surprised, and just let him sleep, in his customary position of arms folded, head back, mouth wide open! I don't know how he did it. I find I can strike the same pose when on the sofa, or so my ex-wife has told me.

I don't remember how Dad and I got back to the car, but I don't think we walked. Wish I could remember who gave us a lift back.

The Le Mans trip I did with my sister's boyfriend, as there was no way my dad would have stuck sleeping on a coach at a racetrack.

As for the racing school trial, I'd need a road licence for that. But a plan came together for that, in a most unexpected way. During 1982 we, as in mum, dad, me and my grandmother went to Florida for a holiday. We went to Ft. Lauderdale near Miami, which I loved. I was very happy to be in America again. But this time not so much mad running around, but we still had adventures.

We. went to Disneyworld and took a trip to the everglades in a huge mobile home with a very strange guy my dad knew. But while I was there, I got to see my old friend from the days when Dad sponsored Tony Dean, the racing driver. His son Richard was over staying with his dad, and being the grafter he was, Richard was working as a car valet at a nightclub, working for tips so he could afford the airfare back. He also did some car jobs for his dad.

I helped him a few times and had great fun with our own adventures. I did my American driving licence course there. It was the easiest driving test ever. At first my dad would let me drive the hire car for about an hour every day for a couple of days until my test. It was a Chevrolet Monte Carlo, and I really liked it. But dad teaching me was hard. He wasn't a great teacher it has to be said, but lucky for me, I did ok and survived without an accident or a fallout. I studied the American highway codebook, and when the day came, off we went. We took a number and waited, but first I did a multiple-choice written exam, which was very easy, and I didn't need to consult my book to jog my memory.

The waiting line was just people sitting outside waiting for the examiner to get out of the last car and call the next number on her list. The examiner had the look on her face that I would learn, many years later, was "instructors' gripe." This is when you see the instructor who had worked with lots of pupils all day, day in day out and was finding it hard to be fresh for the next driver to sit with, and not feel knackered.

Just before I was called the examiner called another number, and a Japanese guy with a silver jacket and mirrored shades stepped forward with his baseball cap on backwards. She checked on her list his name, and asked him to lead her to his car, they got in a white Pontiac Trans-am with a huge bonnet blister for the air filter with the words 6.6 Litre Turbo written on the side, with a large gold eagle on the rest of the bonnet. If first impressions were anything to go by, this could be interesting. And it was, dad and I watched in amazement as the guy reversed out of his space, and wheel spun his way out of the parking lot, with one arm out dangling out of the window for good measure. And dad's immortal line was "well, that's a fail right there isn't it Scotty?" and we both laughed.

But that wasn't the end of it, after only a short time, they returned, and in the parking area there was a rope and coned off area for parallel parking. Mr. Wheelspin couldn't do it! We saw the obviously heated conversation in the car, everyone could as the lazy, quiet queue looked on. Before the examiner got out and Wheelspin's friend went over to drive the car away, with a very pissed off ex-driver sheepishly getting in the passenger seat. Great, I've got to go after that one!

I was called. Dad squeezed my arm, gave me a wink and said, "you'll be fine!"

I lead the lady to my more normal car, told her my name and off we went. I found out the course was very short. I only had to observe the speed limit, stop at a stop sign, indicate left, drive about 1000 yards, and do an emergency stop. Carry on, turn left again, pull into the car park again and parallel park. I did as asked, and at the end the examiner said, "Where are you from?" I told her England. She then said, "Well, you're probably the best driver I've had all day. Congratulations, you passed. Here is the certificate to go and get your licence. Have a nice day!"

I said thank you as she left the car. I moved the car to my original space and got out. Dad came over.... "Well?" he said with his hands out and clearly keen to find out.

"I passed!" I told him.

"Oh! Scotty, I knew you would, and the parking was spot on."

It was a great moment, and one that even now as I write makes me cry out of reliving the moment and reminds me, he's not here anymore.

But that licence was now paving the way to the trial at Brands Hatch racing School. My dad would often remind me who taught me to drive, though I used to tease him about how America didn't count.

Dad only came to my first day at Brands Hatch to see me get my certificate. I carried on at the school from '82 up to early '84. But my mum became the one who drove me to the circuit from after that, and eventually, I'd be driving myself there too. And keep in mind until mid '83, I was still at school. I was 17 but down a year for reasons of the change between the north and south with normal classes too when I joined the stage school. Which was ok and probably the best idea at the time. I tended to drive myself to school with my mum beside me, who would then take my car back home, and meet me later at the end of school, outside. But when I left school in 1983, I had a gap of a few months.

Then I started to work for dad, we had just bought the Hippo-drome, or as it was called then "The talk of the town." It was a legendry variety club in the 50s and 60s and even survived into the early 70s. But it had closed down and been dormant for a fair few years. And now my Dad was having the insides completely ripped out as he turned it into a huge disco venue.

I started with menial jobs like, a door survey, which was lit-erally counting every door in the place from the basement up. I'd note where on the set of building plans it was, what type of door it was single or double wood or metal and measured each door, too. This took a long time. I also cleaned out some storerooms, cleaned the emergency backup batteries of which there were 50 of, before moving on to helping the lighting crews with making the lighting rigs with rivets and checking fuses etc.

The whole place was a building site inside. I didn't see Dad much as I was always on the floor doing some job. Some-times I would see him from a distance wandering around with one of the planning guys with plans and pointing at stuff. I wasn't really included in anything major, just different small jobs. But eventually the club took shape, it was very space age style inside. So much so was dad's vision that he was originally going to call the place "Space". He had all the artwork done, and menus designed.

He was all good to go, but just as the sign out front was being measured, he changed everything. He said he had a very vivid dream about the name, and he woke up suddenly sure that calling it "Space" wasn't right. Recently during the cleaning up of the outside of the venue some very old posters were found embedded in the walls, and they were of historical interest. So, historians were called in and very carefully removed the old posters that dated back as far as its opening of 1889. We even kept some of the posters, of which I now have a couple of. But Dad quite clearly realized that he should give its old original name back, which was "The Hippodrome" and using the statue of the roman charioteer with horses on the top of the building as inspiration, the logo was born. He felt a lot better about the naming after that.

 He'd had another moment of an epiphany before while he was designing the logo for Stringfellows. Again, he had artwork showing versions of options on the themes of his previous clubs with small silhouettes of the top hat man and lady in 20's style, or a cocktail glass alongside the name, or champagne glass... But while mulling these things over at home once at his desk which was like an extension of his work office but was set in the dining room of our home. He also had framed pictures of pinned butterflies on the walls. It was a collection he had slipped into when visiting antique shops with mum. And it struck him then that the logo should be a butterfly, because the club was for "social butterflies". And so the logo for Stringfellows was born.

Back in 1983 I was in employment, and together with a dedicated team of workers the Hippodrome came together. Before the end of the year we were up and running.

The 17th November 1983 was the opening night with Dad, the fronting showman, and I was in the lighting department working the huge "Super Trooper" spotlights for acts that were put on late in the evening. Dad went full pelt back into being club disco and variety venue, as he had got the huge dance floor and put the hydraulic raising stage back into service. The lighting was outstanding with a false ceiling to cover the part of the club that would have pushed the budget too far to recondition to its former glory, which was the gods, as they were known. But this served a purpose of giving room for the gigantic lighting rigs that were going to move up and down and open out over people's heads. It was spectacular when it was all out running and flashing, while there was also laser lighting that was innovative as it came straight from the pioneers in America in water cooled laser technology for clubs.

But on the opening night, we had to open with all the lighting in open static display as the London Council had decreed until we had a health and safety officer free to ratify the safety of our lights moving above people, we couldn't have them moving. The big reveal was delayed, and dad even explained to all the sea of guests that filled the club about that, it still burned him that he couldn't do his light show how he wanted it to happen on the first night.

Pretty soon after the checks, we were allowed to do exactly how dad envisaged it. Even though an inspector came in during the day to check the strength and safety of the laser. As the smoke machine was not allowed to be used to pick out the light better, because the guy thought it would diminish the results, he stood with our resident DJ Peter Tyler on the raised stage after Peter had put the lasers into a static position, so the measuring meter could be used.

The guy asked where one was, so Pete put his hand out found a bright glow on the back of his hand and lead it up to the meter in the guy's hand... he looked, and said, "Oh no that's way too dangerous! That could burn someone's eye" which kind of told you how crap the equipment was, as Pete's hand was fine. So they came to an agreement: that as the lights were always going to be moving, if the equipment was in the "Scan" position, which means it flickers very quickly, that should be alright. Council officials always seem to know what's best though they are not really experts in anything technical.

The club became a great venue for seeing new musical acts and some of the big ones made an early showing at the Hippodrome, like "Frankie Goes to Hollywood", who did their hit song called "Relax" which got banned on radio. But they came and did their song, in the top of the pops style. Dad knew they did a raunchier version for gigs away from the cameras, and that's the one he wanted. So, he made them come back a second time and do their "sexy" version.

 We also had the famed dance troop "Hot Gossip" as our resident entertainment for about three months to play a set every night at 12 a.m. I did the follow spots for that. And when Michael Jackson did his "Thriller" masterpiece video, we used to play that at 1 a.m. every night too. But we also got the odd special gig, like when the group Culture Club came to do a live satellite link up for the American Grammy Awards. I was one of two follow spot operators for that.

The group with Boy George up front were doing a mime to a recording for that. We rehearsed it a few times, just to be sure it ran smoothly, and at the end of the song the group came to the front of the stage and waved to America. So, the link was timed to perfection, we could hear over the speakers in the club that they were going live to London. England for nominee band Culture club play their hit song "Karma Chameleon." And off we went, they mimed perfectly and pranced around the stage under the wonderful Hippodrome lights, and as planned they finished the song and went to front of stage to wave to America... But I forgot about that bit, and as they got to front of stage, I cut my light! And into semi-darkness they plunged! Bugger!

They stayed around for however long it took before the other nominees were read out. When the group "Def Leopard" were read out in the listing, there was a roar from the audience all the way over in the USA that we all heard. Right then George knew they hadn't won as he shrugged his shoulders and retreated from the stage... which of course he was right, the award went to the other English band the aforementioned Def Leopard.

Meanwhile as packing up was in progress, I got a severe bollocking for screwing up the end from my Dad. Some would have thanked me, but not from dad on a live link with the most prestigious music awards gig of the year. And afterwards, I quietly got on with moving cabling and tidying up my lighting station. But while I was doing this Dad had put some music on and was talking with one of his image team who had a night of her own on Thursdays. She was a pink haired lady called Frizzby Fox (not her real name, but her stage name).

I just got on with my work, but then I looked down from my follow spot station which was up on the club's second layer balcony, and I saw dad dancing slowly and very close to the lady. So closely I saw him grabbing her bum and kissing her... I had not known at the time that my dad was having a raging affair with her. And it was Frizzby who saw me looking down and froze! My dad was still married to my mum, and this was a bit of a shock to me.

Frizzby obviously told dad, as he turned around. I stopped staring, and decided it was time for me to go. I started to walk away as I could feel the tears and short, hard breaths coming on... Where I was going, I had no idea. I just wanted to be out of there. But dad was coming after me.

I had never seen Dad being intimate with anyone but my mum before, and it wasn't until a lot later on that I learned that he had a bit of a certain reputation, and a somewhat lax approach to marriage.

Dad caught up with me, but I didn't want to talk to him. But he made me go sit with him in the large exclusive seating area that we called the "Royal Box". He wanted me to ask any questions I might have... I think I only had one.... "why?"

He took a moment or two to collect his thoughts, and how best to reply... and then he said "Well, people change, and I find her very interesting!"

This was his opening gambit, and it was a bit of a kick in the head, to be honest. I know my half-sister was very young when dad left her mum. And I'd always accepted her as my sister, but this was.... different. Well, for me. As it turned out, dad was a bit of a serial philanderer, nobody underage, thank god. But my dad was living a very exciting and magnetic lifestyle that some women were very attracted to, and like-wise, hard for him to pass up the opportunities that must have presented themselves over the years. But now I'd just found out my dad was with another woman.

Turns out my mum knew what was going on, and in her own persuasive way, she did get the lady to sod off for a while at least, but things would change a few years later.

It has to be said that at age 18, I was an adult, and should be dealing with life's little surprises. Although I knew it wasn't Frizzby fully at fault, though she should have not carried on with a very prominent figure and who also was married. I still wouldn't talk to her. After my mum and dad's divorce a couple of years later, I still kept a bit of a distance, but ac-cepted things a bit better.

Back at the club I was also struggling with the work hours, even though my hours now are way worse. At 18 I was not eating right, discovering beer and martini, and generally sleeping most of the day. It was a case of eat, work, sleep, repeat. But some days I was still going to Brands Hatch to do some time chasing lapping. I did the Brands Hatch School in house races too, driving one of their fleet of Fiat X-19's. I was terrible. I couldn't get on with the car and finished up 22nd in the closed championship.

It was racing, but not real racing as far as I was concerned. Into 1984 I convinced dad to come with me to the annual racing car show held in London in January of that year. It was nice to mooch round the small show that back then was held at the Cunard Centre out Hammersmith way. I was very keen to look at the manufactures' section, where all the car makers were. I saw Reynard, Van Diemen and Lola who were the three main makers of the FF1600s which was outside of Karting, every driver's racing ladder starting point. While looking and in some cases, sitting in the cars, we got a lot of interest. Clearly, dad was recognised, and completely obvious that his son was a bit racing car crazy. It wasn't long before he was approached by a few guys who were drivers.

I got hustled into the Van Diemen RF84 to sit in by a very enthusiastic Irish chap who turned out to be Tommy Byrne, a man who was knocking on the door of F1 at the time and had driven his Van Diemen to victory many a time and had won the British F3 championship in 1982. Next a lad I recognised, Julian Bailey introduced himself to dad, and I'd seen him win the Formula Ford Festival at Brands Hatch in 1982. Julian actually asked dad if he'd be interested in sponsoring him, and to my absolute amazement, dad told him that if he was going to sponsor anyone, it was going to be his son...

This was the first-time dad had even mentioned the idea, I was just doing the school and did want to race, but no idea how I was going to get started. Here was my answer, without my even asking too! We then got talking to Reynard Racing Cars. And I liked the look of the Reynard better too. On the stand we got talking to a guy who asked us if one of their works drivers could have a stag doo at the Hippodrome and if we could come to an arrangement over the cost of the small gathering by offsetting it against a test at Silverstone in a Reynard 84FF FF1600. Which was great, but Dad didn't come to watch that, which was a shame. It was the first time I'd used my racing licence outside of Brands Hatch as the test was on the Silverstone short track.

Meanwhile back in the real world, or club land, I was still drifting into a strange existence. Also, at this time my girlfriend moved in with us at the family home in London. I think it was to help her get to more modelling jobs with better ease. And then a lot of things happened very quickly.

I took a break from working at the club as I was getting ill from not eating right and not going out much during the day. And the girlfriend moved out as living with me, my mum and dad was something she couldn't handle, I think. But life goes on, and I got reminded about the F3 driver Russell Spence who was going to have his stag doo at the Hippodrome. Which was good because that opened talks about racing for real with a team that Russell and the Reynard guys knew.

This led me to race for a team based in Grantham, Lincolnshire called Richard Dutton Racing, and I don't even remember if I did an official test with them. But I remember the conversation with dad about it.

Dad was concerned about my safety, just like any other protective parent. Until now I'd just be going to Brands Hatch and doing some laps, the real test with another team I did at Silverstone was the real carrot, and I had got a taste of a car that wasn't a tired school racing car. But here I was trying to do some real races in the latter half of 1984 with an established team.

Richard was already running a few drivers, one in FF1600 (who would be my teammate), one in FF2000, one in S2000, one in British F3 and a guy in a saloon car, also a rally car. Dad was quite impressed that this guy Richard was running so many cars, other than sponsoring Tony Dean and a one-off race in 1983 for David Hunt in a Formula 3 race, dad didn't know anything about the business of racing. As far as he was concerned it was just a hobby that people did, rich older people with sons and daughters that were just doing it for fun.

Dad's whole life was about the clubs and although he had good knowledge about many things, motor racing wasn't one of them. But he met Richard and felt he was a good man, and though dad was going to be financing my start into the real motor racing world, there wasn't going to be any logos on the car. Just my name of the side and an off the shelf racing suit and helmet. All dad asked of Richard... "just keep my son safe." And away I went.

This was the start of the life I wanted, since the age of 5, according to my grandmother, I'd said I wanted to be a racing driver when I grew up. And here I was, about to start my journey in another world, but not so sure about the grown-up bit.

I went to Snetterton in my Suzuki Jeep, which felt like forever as it was also the longest trip I had driven on my own in my car which was not even a 1000 CC's. I did a test on the Friday in a white Lola FF1600 which was to be my car. The next day I qualified somewhere near the back, but not last. I started my first race, but at the first corner I got involved with someone else's crash, then I carried on.

Hit the brakes for the second corner and the car turned sharp left and took me into the turnip field just before the corner.

End of race. So, though I was sad that mum and dad wasn't there for my first race, I was also pleased they weren't too. In 1984 there were no mobiles, so the first chance I got to tell them what happened was when I got back home that same night. I do think my dad hoped that I would soon give up if my results weren't good. But this is when I discovered a lot about my relationship with dad now that I was, in the eyes of the law, an adult.

7

PULLING IN DIFFERENT DIRECTIONS

The relationship between a father and son is like a constantly flowing river: it moves along its way and sometimes slows, sometimes comes to what seems like a stop, but still meanders through life with the odd fast section. My dad and I were close, but sometimes miles apart. As I started to develop as a young man, I started to see dad in a new way, and I'm not talking about him and women or anything like that.

This is nothing new to the world. This is how relationships go. Losing closeness with your father can happen, mainly because of choices we make, and I mean that for both father and son. Developing your own tastes is a test for both, music is usually the start. However, in our case, we didn't have that problem. I liked a lot of the music he liked, and though he never said, didn't seem to mind if I was playing my favourite Genesis or Eric Clapton stuff. We never had any problems in choice of TV programs either, while I was still living at the family home anyway. He just accepted what I liked was what I liked and never pulled me down about it. And even though I'm sure he didn't want me to get too involved with the motor racing world, he never stopped or discouraged me. Sure, later on when I got to the age he thought I should step back and do some real work!

We didn't have any real problems, nothing that resulted in not speaking to each other. But from 1984 and for the next five years while racing, and a bit longer if you count the motor racing instructing I did for 21 years, we didn't see much of each other.

Actually, in truth, I didn't leave home, it was more my family left me. Ok that's not quite true, but it seemed like that as I went to live up north for about two years to be near the racing team, and then I came back to my dad having left my mum with divorce proceedings on the way. Then my mum and I moved out to outside of London only for her to meet a guy in America, get married and moved out there. But the thing about the early racing years '84- '85, I was in a unique position of going home back to mum and dad after races, but also back to my sponsor.

Unlike many racing fathers, he didn't come to many races, and when he did come, he was there to be social, and not get in the middle of team talks or giving advice. He just came to see his son race. Which was great, however, he missed all my firsts. My first race, my first top 6 finishing position that came at Brands Hatch. My first podium and 3rd place trophy, which was also the first trophy I ever got for anything. My first win, or any win!

I look back and would trade everything for him to see me win a race. Well, everything but my kids.

The year wore on, I was learning a lot about racing, and about life outside the protection of the family from being in a school where everyone around me was into the same thing. This became my university, being with people who loved racing as much as me was brilliant.

But there were still some people that were quick to judge just like the old mixed interests' schools. And more people around that knew who my dad was, and I was quickly dubbed as a "playboy" just because I jumped straight into cars and wasn't from the usual karting background like so many of my fellow racers.

My learning curve was so steep I needed crampons and a rope. But it didn't deter me, I was living my dream, and it was wonderful. Meanwhile, dad had been going from strength to strength and was now in his hay day of notoriety. The Hippodrome was doing very well, so well that dad started Hippodrome Records, which he put my mum in charge of.

That meant he could still indulge in his music-related dream of managing a successful artist. He developed a showcase of music night, and also reintroduced the format of the "gong show" which was acts coming on stage, doing their bit, and if they weren't deemed good enough by the audience, they were given the cue to get off stage by a large gong being sounded to indicate they had to leave the stage.... which funnily enough sounds a lot like the X factor now. Back in 1984 Simon Cowell used to manage the odd act and used to come in the club back then too.

I wonder if we gave him an idea?

By the end of '84 dad was running two very successful clubs and I'd done about 20 races in three months.

I was also about to make a very bad decision but wouldn't realise until about a year later. My new racing friend who had his stag doo at the Hippodrome earlier that year, and had pointed me towards Richard Dutton, proposed an idea to me.

For 1985, he said I should get out of the Dutton team and start my own. He had a friend who would be a great team manger to run the team (as luck would have it) call it Hippodrome Racing, just me in the team, no teammates.

Get a brand-new Reynard chassis, and get a garage unit based at Silverstone to run it from. Obviously to anyone with a brain would see this was trying to run before you can walk.

But I had the rose-coloured glasses on, and the thought of having a team and car with Hippodrome all over it really appealed. He sold me the idea really well. So, I told Richard my plan, and to be fair to him he tried to make me see sense, but I was already brainwashed.

In wonderful technicolour hindsight, I should have stayed put with Dutton and developed my driving more. But I was green as hell, easily swayed and my dad was going to finance it all as getting exposure outside of London appealed to him. Also, I was his son, and he wanted me to be happy I suppose. The wheels were set in motion... I should have smelled a rat when after the first meeting with my new manager he had a two-year-old VW Golf GTi, after the first payment of sponsorship to set everything up, with car, unit, and a small truck. He suddenly had an almost new Audi Quattro, which in 1984-85 was the car to have. But my crook radar wasn't even plugged in, let alone switched on. I was 19 and very excited.

The unit was small and cheap, nothing wrong with that, the truck was small and more than second hand, but that was alright too. I found out later the chassis was free from Reynard, a brand-new Reynard 85FF. The engine deal, I never knew the status of, but it was by one of the best builders at the time, Minister Engines. It was a lovely black car, with a huge sign with large lettering of HIPPODROME down both sides of it and the truck.

The money spent must have been a lot, but that wasn't my department. I just had to drive, and that was all I wanted to do. Somehow for the first race of the year, we had number 1 on the car. I've still yet to find the programme from the meeting with me at the top of the entry list, but knowing now what my manager was like, it was probably too late for registration to be included in the programme.

It didn't matter, I was first out of the pits at qualifying at Brands Hatch on the Grand Prix circuit which I'd only driven on the previous day for the first time on practice day. I scampered off, completely forgetting about cold tyres on the first lap, maybe because I wanted to be first past the pits. But come the second until last corner I slid off the track and damaged my car and ultimately the chassis, which we couldn't fix. So first out, first off, first home! Great start to the year, and I still had yet to drive home and tell my dad/sponsor the news, which was hard.

That led to me getting a small flat in a village between Silverstone and Oxford. It was a very cheap one bed/lounge, kitchen and bathroom place in Abingdon. This was my first home away from home, I guess.

1985 was a challenging year in many ways. My relationship with my girlfriend was being strained, and I was seeing less of my mum and dad too.

I was stretching my wings, creating my own life, while dad was looking to stretch his further too. I didn't know it at the time until later in the year, but he was looking across the pond, mainly at New York. The call of America was gathering strength again. And throughout this year he was working hard on making it happen. Meanwhile, I was learning more tracks, and that my car wasn't as good as the others. I don't mean that because the results weren't coming, I mean that because we discovered it had a handling problem.

If anything, it sharpened my reflexes up as it darted left and right under braking. But later in the year, we went to Oulton Park in Cheshire. Not a million miles away from where we used to live, funny how life sometimes loops round into your past. In this race, I started well for once. It was a junior championship. Three quarters way round the track into a corner called Druids Bend, a quick double apex corner, some idiot left it a little late to have a go at me, realised it and pulled out of the manoeuvre a little too late.

We touched wheels quite hard and round both he and I went, but like Snetterton the year before I carried on, and like the previous year I discovered a problem with the car at the very next corner. I braked, but nothing happened, and my car carried on at something like 100 miles an hour, I started to spin as I tried to make the corner. As I did so the car swapped ends, and probably just as well too as a front impact would have been very bad as this time there was no turnip field, just a tire wall and strong metal barrier behind that. As the car spun it slowed a little which was good, however I still slammed backwards into the wall. The next thing I knew I had marshals and medics climbing all over the car. I was clearly in a bit of trouble as I wasn't able to get out, and my back and neck ached.

After careful extrication by the brilliant Oulton Park marshals and back to the medical centre, it was found I must just have a bit of neck and back bruising. I felt like shit, and as a pre-caution, a trip to Northampton general was in order. My team manager took me along, leaving my mechanic and his helper to shuffle the broken car into the truck.

Unsurprisingly my manager was not sympathetic, he was more pissed off with having to go to a hospital than go home, and though I can't remember how long it took, I'm sure it wasn't a huge wait. And the x-rays showed I was fine, just bruising and time at home resting was in order. Meanwhile back at home, some kind soul had rung my mum and dad to tell them I'd had a shunt but was ok, and not to worry.

Great thanks, up until then there was no worry, now there was lots of worry, the world still wasn't wired up with mobile phones and internet was still in its infancy. I got back home in London to face a barrage of questions... Why had they heard from a marshal and not my manager? What would have happened if things were worse? Dad, the sponsor wasn't in the room at this point, Dad "the dad" was in charge. But typically, because he hadn't seen the accident, he was calmer than my mum, who was living all the scenarios in her head from the moment she heard to my standing there.

I ached all over as the bruising was more severe than I was making out. Funny how Dad never actually threatened to pull the plug then, but I think my mum was hoping he would.

It's true to say my dad had a selfish side, but he was very caring too, to many people, not just me and family. He could also detach himself because he lived in his own world of club life, and no interest in anything else, and racing cars he couldn't really connect with. On the one hand he was detached without interfering at the tracks when he turned up but didn't think about any of it if he wasn't there at all. It was sometimes frustrating, but also a relief at the same time.

'85 moved on and I was back at the wheel, and struggling on, my results sporadic but not great. Later in the year, I got picked up by the guys from my house to go testing at Snetterton, I'd woken at 4:30 in the morning and we were off at 5 a.m. A full day of belting around Snetterton from 9 until about 4:30 p.m. before we packed up and drove all the way back to Abingdon back to my flat, I had to go do some food shopping, then out to take my new girlfriend out to dinner, as Sarah and I had split up earlier that summer.

On the way out to dinner I had a minor accident with another car on a wet road, addresses were exchanged. Later on, I was so tired I let my girlfriend drive my car back to her house, where she lived with her mum and dad. She had a licence as we were both 19, and I think protected under my insurance.

At her house I asked if I could stay on the sofa, but she thought her mum and dad wouldn't like it. I said I'd sleep in my car, that was a no go either, she lived in Whittlebury, which wasn't far from Silverstone track where my workshop was. If I had been more with it, I should have parked up at the unit and slept there, but no... I decided in my infinite wisdom to drive back to Abingdon, which wasn't that far... now was it?

On the way, I stopped at a little chef, which was a roadside eating place I knew, and though it was shut, I put my seat back and dozed off for a bit. The engine was on, heater going, and Madonna played on the cassette machine. I had a really fun Mini MG metro turbo at this time, and I loved it.

I woke up and thought I would be ok to get home now... I was wrong. I woke up bouncing along the grass beside the road, and instinctively turned the wheel to get back on, but it had been raining. The car headed back towards the road ok, except it was going sideways and spinning slowly round as I got back to the pavement. I slewed onto the road, no idea at what speed, but in the wet it doesn't make much difference and inertia takes over.

I was heading for a tree on my side, but I had enough intelligence to try do something about it, I whipped the handbrake on to make the car spin round some more to try flip it round to the other side, if I was going to hit something it needed to be the other side, it worked, and though I hit the kerb too, the car popped up into the air and landed sideways into a solid tree.

I yelled as I hit. Miraculously I was unhurt but trapped in the car as my car was bent round the tree, and my door was bent round too. But I could move around, and Madonna was still playing on the car stereo. I can't listen to "Like a virgin" without remembering the accident. I found the front windscreen had popped out in one piece, so I climbed out the gaping hole. I had put my hazard lights on, and then went to the road to flag anyone down. Two cars passed, but I must have looked like a drunk, so I can't blame them for carrying on. The third car stopped, I told him what happened, and he kindly went off to get the police, who were great.

I didn't need an ambulance thankfully. And after the car was taken away, my alarm on my watch went off just as the police were taking me back home, and I managed to call my team manager. This was 24 hours later, and the reason I'd crashed was obvious, I had been awake for 22 of them. My manager let me use his car to get myself back home to London since he had another car, so I was grateful for that.

There I was driving his Audi Quattro, we had probably paid for, back home, but the fun hadn't stopped, as like a complete dummy I got stopped for speeding. 100 miles an hour in a 70 on the M40. Doh!

The conversation with mum and dad was another round of the previous one, but with added fun with the speeding, which I didn't tell them about until much later in the evening. Again, my mum imagined the possible outcomes, and dad again looking distant as I was clearly ok.

After that episode I got a new car, I don't know how I convinced them, but I got a Ford Escort XR3i, that was almost like getting the fabled VW Golf Gti, but not quite.

Dad was brilliant, and I knew how lucky I was to have such a dad through all of this. My racing exploits were not going as well as I hoped, but typical for me I was my own worst critic.

The annual formula Ford festival came along, and it was a cracker of a meeting, 242 cars were entered. I was feeling hopeful that I'd do ok. I wanted to reach the final as it was a set of heats, quarters, and semi-finals spread over 3 days. I managed to get myself into one of the quarterfinals for the last day, and with that, my mum and dad were coming to watch. But when I got to the track and my team manager saw me, he said "your famous today".

I was a bit puzzled, but he showed me the centre pages of The Sun newspaper. In large letters over two not so flattering pictures of dad and I, the banner headline "Oddfellows", some moronic journalist had decided to do a hatchet job of an article to show us up. I can't remember the full gist of the piece, but I was suddenly reminded of the school days of other such revelations that were the next day's chip shop paper, all in the name of selling a newspaper.

Strangely it didn't have the same effect as those school days, I was older, tougher and understood more. I did just what dad did... ignored it and carried on. And to be honest, so did everyone else that I knew in the paddock. If anything, we all had a laugh at it. I'm sure one or two people took the view of me being a laughingstock, but there will always be people like that. I think it's a form of jealousy.

I'd learned that it really didn't change much, as my dad was my sponsor, so didn't affect my standing, and he too laughed at it, in fact, he loved it as he would say "Scotty, being talked about is one thing, but not being talked about is quite another." He knew exactly how to play the press.

I just missed out on getting into the semi-finals, but that was fine. I ended up watching the rest of the races in a hospitality suite eating and drinking with friends while watching history being made as Johnny Herbert beat all the odds to win in a car made by a very small manufacturer called Quest Cars.

Bertrand Gachot, who was a works driver for Van Diemen, had a monumental crash where his helmet was close to scraping on the floor as he was flipped at the first corner of his semi-final. Both Herbert and Gachot would go on to win at Le Mans in the famous 24-hour race, and both got to Formula 1. Also, in the final that year, and came third was future world champion Damon Hill. So, I was in good company on my racing ladder.

I parted company with my team manager soon after and also nearly gave up completely, but my old friend Richard Dean, whom was also racing in FF1600 that year, introduced me to

Jim Lee, who ran him that year and together they had won the Star of Mallory Championship. I got a chance to test with Jim not too long later, which was a fabulous day and I agreed I'd run with him for 1986, as long as my dad was ok with it.

This was going to be another test of my relationship with dad, as we had found that running our own team was very, very expensive. And he was starting to see that the racing bug wasn't going away.

However, I highlighted to him that this team I wanted to join wasn't anything like our own team, which as it turned out was exploited financially by the team manager. He had pulled some right stunts in our name. I was right about the first payment going to him and his next car as I found out the Reynard chassis was free, and after I had a chassis damaging accident, the car was stripped down to its bare chassis with no bits on, which I helped to do because I was learning about the mechanics of a car at the same time.

That was thrown out the back on a tip. The manager had already taken the chassis plate off the car, and in my naivety, I had asked to have it, but he said no as he wanted it for his "collection". What I didn't know was that a brand-new chassis was being shoved his way through the back door of Reynard's and the plate would find its way onto that. I think that as they had made so many chassis but weren't selling them well because the car wasn't great, the odd one could get... lost.

Also, the managers costs were very inventive let's say. I was later to find out the amount of money that went his way was nearly twice that of a full works team budget for a year. I did enter a lot of races, and on one memorable day I did 4 qualifying sessions for 4 races. Which led one chief paddock marshal at the track to ask... "don't they let you out of the car then?"

If dad had been to more races, and been a bit more hands-on, he might have spotted something I wasn't looking for. I nearly gave up, but I was rescued by both my friend Richard, my Dad's huge generosity and liking that I was tenacious about going racing.

He, like many, liked a fighting underdog, which I suppose I was. The pressure of being a "son of" with our club logo written large on my car, my racing suit and helmet was big, but I wanted to succeed.

Dad decided we would go for it again. And this time I'd avoid the major championships to see if I could do better. Dad met Jim Lee and liked him right away. Jim was respectful of people like my dad, people who made their way of life a success and became notable for it. Jim was a down to earth Yorkshireman, and he promised he would "keep Scotty safe".

The end of 1985 was going to be notable for something else, but we didn't know it at the time. I have a photograph from Christmas day around the dinner table. All the family are there. Mum and her mother, my sister and her boyfriend (who turned into an arse, unfortunately) my dad's mum and dad, me but no girlfriend as we had broken up just before Christmas, and my dad at the head of the table. It's a great picture and poignant because this would be the last time we were all together.

8

ON TRACK TO WINNING FOR BOTH OF US

A fresh start to the new year was in order.

After Christmas, it was a crazy evening at the Hippodrome for New Year's Eve. It was rammed with people, and I was hopeful of a better year. I wanted to get away from England for a bit and it was decided that I would go to Florida in America and stay with my mate Richard in Fort Lauderdale at his dad's house out there with him.

I was packed off with a healthy amount of spending money and went to have a great time with Richard. We did all sorts, which also included frequenting an outdoor kart circuit in the warm evenings, where both Richard and I frequently sliced our way through other drivers to end up leading the whole lot of them by the end of the session, it was like testing. And I wished my dad had come out with me for the fun, but I had just turned 20, and dad was busy with his next big project. He himself was jet setting to and from the USA, full of fresh ideas and working on building a new nightclub, this time in New York.

I took off from Miami airport on the same day that the space shuttle Challenger had exploded on its way up and killed all on board. Driving to the airport I saw so many cars with their headlights on in daylight as part of an outpouring of respect for the lost astronauts. I returned home to get fit in time for the start of the season, and just before my first race of the year my dad was ready to open his new club.

I had recently got back with Sarah, so we went together to the opening of Stringfellows New York. This was literally a couple of days before my first race of 1986 at Oulton Park. We were chauffeured into Manhattan from the airport by a great chauffeur called Curtis. We were in the New York Hilton, it was great. And the opening a smashing success, just a shame we had to get back to England for my race, I could have quite happily stayed with Sarah there for a week at least.

On the flight back I was a bit of a twit and not much fun as I just wanted to get some sleep because I didn't want to feel jet-lagged for the race. As soon as we returned, I dropped her off at her mum's, I was away off north. It was again another event without mum or dad, obviously, they were still in New York.

This first race was the Champion of Oulton championship and was another one of those I'd wished my dad had seen, as I fought for a step on the podium so hard that I drove around the outside of the guy in 3rd place who would turn out to be my main foe in the championship for the rest of the year, this bold manoeuvre lead to me getting my first trophy for anything.... ever. The joy of having the right car, a good team and a good result straight away at the start of the year was wonderful, but also tempered by the sadness that none of my family was there to see it. Nor even my girlfriend, as she didn't want to go all the way up north.

That would spell the real end of my relationship with Sarah. It was a sad situation as we had been together since stage school. I wanted her to take to racing, but she couldn't, the modelling work and life came first for her. And I had my own road to follow.

A few more races followed in both Champion of Oulton and Star of Mallory, each one another podium and a step closer to a win. We decided to do an extra race somewhere else, and Donnington was chosen. I qualified very well in 3rd behind yet two more main championship guys, so I was hopeful of another 3rd because I was about a second down on them. If you're not a motorsport person you won't know that's a lot and known as "being off the pace". But on the first lap, they started pulling away by the 3rd corner, so I was resigned for that 3rd which was ok with me, but then heading into the tight Esses Chicane ahead of me I saw the two cars fighting over first touch and both spin out either side in the middle of the corner, I picked my way through the pair and suddenly realised... I was leading! Fuck.... what do I do now?

The guy behind me obviously sensed my trepidation and tried to get alongside before the hairpin bend coming up. But I recovered and just got on with it, because the guy behind me was a regular at the Mallory races, so I wasn't afraid of him. And over the course of the race I kept my lead, and even though one of the guys who had the off had recovered and was catching me, he didn't quite make it even though he broke the lap record trying.

On the slowing down lap tears streamed down my face, which I couldn't wipe away as I had a helmet and flameproof balaclava on. But I was shouting out to my dad that I'd won! It was a joyful yet hard moment.

I took my time to get back to the pits. I took off my helmet once I'd stopped and quickly wiped my face with my balaclava. Jumped out of the car to receive a flower garland but no trophy, they didn't have one, which has always annoyed me. Jim Lee was as close to a dad reaction as I was going to get. He did his best, but it wasn't dad. The win was almost empty for him not being there.

More wins came after that, it was like I'd found the magic ingredient, and suddenly there was no stopping me. If I didn't win, I was usually in the top 3.

1986 was a rollercoaster of a year. Outside of the tracks other stuff jumped up to surprise me. I knew my mum and dad's marriage was in a bad way, and somewhere in that year dad moved out and went to live at the Savoy hotel for a while until he found somewhere, he liked to live. Which was hard to deal with, but also at the same time my mum's mother was dying of cancer.

I wasn't happy that dad moved out while mum was going through all that. I was living near the team up north at the time, sharing a flat with Richard Dean, but I got into the habit of driving down to London when I wasn't testing to go visit my Nannan. It was heart-breaking to see her slipping away, and still dad and mum kept up a pretence that all was ok for her mother.

In truth, my mum was dealing with two of the hardest things in life for anyone. A marriage breakup and the death of her mother. It also affected me. My results took a tumble for a bit. I stopped winning and I knew it was with all the things that were going on outside of the track that were leaking into my mind when driving. I had to do something about it. I took to being logical and trained myself to leave my problems at the entrance gates, while at the circuit and on track there was nothing I could do about my problems or worries.

It was more productive to just think about nothing but the car and track, and the business of winning the race. This was how I created an escape. Worrying about my grandmother while on track wasn't going to change anything or help her. Same with my mum and dad's marriage. Before I came along, they were just two different people who liked each other enough to get very close and decide to make a go of it. People change and that's life.

With this new way of thinking I got back to my winning ways and went on to lead both the championships I was con-centrating on. I still was driving up and down the M1 to see my grandmother who wasn't improving, and my own mother was right by her side. I slipped into a kind of routine, testing, visit my grandmother, race at the weekend... repeat!

During all of this time I saw little of my dad, but he did come to a race at Oulton Park. I don't remember who he was with, but I know it wasn't Frizzby. But he stood next to Richard when the race was on. A race I should have won, I was on pole position, but the second-place guy on the grid got the jump on me. I followed this guy closely for the entire race, up until the last lap, where I took a long lunge down the inside going into the hairpin... but I had left my move a little too late and locked up the right front wheel which made me slide straight on, he carried on and I recovered to keep 2nd place as we were so far ahead of the other drivers. I was gutted, I was so close to winning in front of my dad.

1986 rolled on and I managed to win both championships. When we went to pick up the trophy for the Champion of Oulton at the BRSCC dinner later in the year, it was a bitter-sweet night. On the same day as the doo, my grandmother had passed away from cancer. But still we went to the awards night. Both Mum and Dad were with me, I have some fantastic pictures from the night, and one with my mum who was doing an amazing job of keeping it together, but you could see she was having a hard time.

The next step after a year of winning in FF1600 was usually FF2000. But Jim and I had an idea, and I had to put it to my sponsor, a.k.a. my Dad.

I proposed that we jump a step and went to British Formula 3, but in the year older cars class known as Class B. It meant a bit of a hike in budget, but as we had spent just slightly less than half the amount that 1985's rip-off season, the little extra was still better than that.

Jim Lee was asking for £90,000 for F3, which I found out later, was bloody good. Dad looked thoughtful across the office table at the Hippodrome. "Scotty you know you could have a very nice car and rent a very nice flat in London for this kind of money," he said.

I beg to differ about the flat, as London was silly money way back then, but he was right about the car.

"Scott, you could have a Porsche and come work properly for me," he emphasized.

Damn, he knew my weak spot. But driving racing cars was way better than tarting around London in a flash car.

"Yes Dad, I'm sure you're right, but this is about trying to get a career in motor racing, and this is a step that isn't that big a jump before F1, and unlike the 1600's, this time we get TV."

This got his attention, and made financial sense to him, here was an opportunity to advertise the club to a wider audience.

He agreed to our proposal, and I would continue to live up near the team even though I'd be all over the country following the F3 circus. I was very excited.

We did a launch at the Hippodrome for the new venture into F3, and also to celebrate the double championship win. We had the car on stage and revealed it to all my guests and customers in the club. I had friends from school days, and racing friends and some of my rivals too.

Some well-known people, like Nick Mason from the band Pink Floyd were there too. Unfortunately racing legend Stirling Moss couldn't make it, and sent a nice letter explaining that he would be at the Swedish motor show that day. But it's a letter I still have and cherish. It was a great way to start the year, and Dad and I were on stage together to show the car and have a bit of banter.

This year dad came to a few races and saw a different kind of atmosphere to the one circuit championships. This time he saw a more international flavour with other big championships running alongside us, which fitted in better with his ideas, though he still didn't get the real side of it being a working sport.

Meanwhile, he was flying between England and New York with his new club open and doing okay. Though I didn't know it at the time, but he was fighting many battles in the states for a foothold in the world of Manhattan, where the town never sleeps, but you have to be tough to survive. This didn't mean London was soft, far from it, but New York was different with new challengers to deal with.

Also, let's not forget that the 17-year-old Peter Stringfellow had been past this way before with the merchant navy in 1957, and really wanted to come back and be a star in his own right.

1987 would come and go in a flash, and I even managed to get a few podiums positions, the more notable ones being when abroad in Holland at Zandvoort circuit with a 3rd, and Spa-Francorchamps also a 3rd and a 2nd place at Donnington. I managed that one even though I'd been to see my favourite music band Genesis in concert at Wembley in London, which was a mad dash up and down the motorway after qualifying 3rd for the race. We did alright for our first step into Formula 3.

1988 was to be a strange year. Something happened that tested both of us.

The year was going well, the car we acquired and my experience developing was making racing look really good. I was visiting the podium a little more, and the opposition in Class B, which I had decided to have another go at, were all good. I was getting a good reputation. But dad was again not at many events, I was a lone wolf with no family or sponsor at the race meetings.

However, I did put my car on 5th overall on a windy day at Silverstone, when I just made the right setting calls on my car, but in the race, I was pushed out and damaged by a couple of class A cars that decided I wasn't really there in the corner with them.

It was a shame, because I knew I could have won that race. Later in the year at the same track, I had a different experience. It was a qualification race as it was the short circuit configuration, and I didn't quite make the main grid, but I was on front row for the qualification race, alongside a class A car. I was determined to win this race because only the first two cars of class B had got into the main race, so I could be on for another podium position if I won this out of the B cars.

But as I made a good start, David Brabham made a better one, and scythed past the class A car behind me by the second corner which was a slow hairpin bend. On the main back straight he was right behind, we were virtually side by side, and then something happened. We touched wheels and my car went sideways at 130 miles per hour. David's car landed on my sidepod, and we speared off the track together. There was no grass only tarmac and metal barrier.

I hit the barrier with full force, so hard it broke the front of my car off and one of my own front wheels hit my helmet, which knocked me out cold. We then bounced out into the track together and across the front of the chasing pack of cars. The race was stopped to extract me from the car.

Now I don't have any memory of this day, and I only know the details now because other people watching told me what actually happened, even David Brabham himself told me what happened, as after this accident we became great close friends. He said it was nobody's fault, we just were both trying to occupy the same bit of track space.

I was taken to hospital, diagnosed with some head bruising and had caused me to have short term memory loss, which lasted about three days. I missed the next round of the championship due to waiting for a new car to be found and doctor's orders.

This led to me convalescing back at home in London with my mum. The accident had several strange effects on me. First, I could only write in capital letters, which went on for about 8 years until my writing began to get back to normal. Second, for 3 days straight, I developed an obsession for writing a series of numbers down, which turned out to be phone numbers of friends, but all the numbers in each were in the wrong order, but the right digits. Third, I was speaking my mind. Fourth, I was angry.

The brain is a strange thing; we still know less about it than most things. We know more about the moon than our own brains and the bottom of the sea. But while I was laid up in my bed with note pad by my side, and a brain fizzing away trying to fill in the gap in my memory, dad had called up and left a message with my mum for me to give him a ring.

"Me ring him?... I'm the one who had the accident." The words just tumbled out of my mouth.

In normal circumstances I would have just rung him back and just assured him I was ok. But I wasn't myself, the thoughts were just queuing up ready in my head and just waiting for the first opportunity to come out. My mum got it straight away, and just said "Okay... I'm sure he'll ring again" and quietly tip-toed out of the room.

I was in a strange state, but I had questions for Dad, and I wasn't going to grovel to him, he had better ring me. Now I'm not the disruptive type, or violent, but I felt an anger within. Which as a racing driver you learn how to channel your aggression into pushing your car with controlled aggression, literally direct your feelings into feeling the car and balancing it in corners and wringing its neck on the straights.

I was genuinely angry about some things and once I came out of my strange way, I felt a little guilty for my words and thoughts. But until that moment, my dad had to ring back. And I'm pretty sure my mum called him up and gave him a gentle warning after the first attempt, just to let him know I wasn't the same as before. How could he know anyway, as by this time dad had moved out, and I didn't see him much. In all honesty, I was an adult at 22 years old and needed to sort myself out.

Because my phone was switched off in my room to give me peace while recovering, my mum let me know that dad was on the line again. I didn't waste time.

"Hi Dad, I'm glad you've rung, because I've got some questions for you!"

"Okay Scott, but how are you after the accident?" dad said in a calm and measured way.

I was straight to the point of the thoughts burning in my head.

"I'm fine, Dad why are you with Frizzby, she's way too young for you, so caked with makeup all the time I can't see what's so great about her, and mum is brilliant... You're an idiot for letting her go!"

There was a moments silence, and I realised we had been down this road before, and the answers were going to be pretty much the same, I just didn't get it. My mind was racing with so many things at once, the accident had taken the social barriers down and I was running riot.

He yet again said that people change, and this is the person he felt he wanted to be with, he had no idea if it would last

MY DAD WAS THE KING OF CLUBS

or not, but this was now, and he was happy with her.... I'd just got to accept that some things in life don't last forever. Though his own mother and father were devoted to each other, he was sure that they must have had days where they could have thrown in the towel. But because of their own poverty, four children to keep and the lack of personal space in their tiny home back in Sheffield many years ago, they didn't have the choice of divorce or even to go anywhere else, but he and my mum had the choice.

I found out soon after my grandmother died it was my mum's choice for him to leave, because she couldn't deal with her mother's steady deterioration and my dad's affair at the same time. She only had some kind of control over one of the predicaments and so asked dad to leave. Which he did. And I knew why he complied and left; so he wouldn't feel the guilt if it wasn't his decision!

This is one of the things I learned about my father, when you learn about the man. I was angry that he didn't just leave Frizzby alone for a while to back up my mum in her time of need, because we all knew my Nannan didn't have long. He should have just been there for her until it was over, then quietly bow out if that was how he felt.

In many ways, the accident made a man of me. It made me confront things that I just ignored or put to the back of my mind. In truth, my Dad wasn't good with other people being ill. When he lost his own mother, I don't know how he dealt with it, as I wasn't around during that time. Though I did visit her way before her own illness got worse.

But then again, my Dad's own dad was still around and so Elsie, my Dad's mum, was being cared for. With my mum's mum, she had lost two husbands to different illnesses years before. My mum and her two older brothers did their best, but it was mainly my mum who did the bulk of the looking after things.

PAGE | 89

As the days past the capitol letter writing thing was driving me mad as I couldn't change it back. My frustration of being cooped up in the house was driving me wild too. And one day I decided to just get out in my car and drive... anywhere. If I got lost... so be it. I didn't have a mobile phone yet and sat-nav was still a long way off.

I slipped some jeans and a t-shirt on, grabbed my keys and wallet, and slipped out of the house without telling mum. I just needed space, and I was sure she wouldn't have let me go. I went for a drive around London. I was fine, like a tonic to get out in my natural habitat, the car. It was while I was out that I cracked what the writing down numbers was about.

When I returned, my mum was on the verge of calling the police and my dad was on the phone again as she had alerted him. But I was calmer than before and in turn, calmed my mum down. I needed to get back in the racing car again.

I spoke to dad again on the phone, and he understood where I was at. Though concerned he got my frustration, I knew I sounded different and better than before, but neither of us brought up the subject of our previous conversation. I knew he would never say anything about it again.

In late summer, an opportunity came up for Dad to actually do a race, a pro-celebrity race. It was at the Brands Hatch meeting for the Formula 3 Super Prix, but he was to drive one of the racing school Ford XR3i's with Paul Warwick as his pro-driver.

Why I wasn't asked, I'll never know. But I had asked for, an got the job of instructing my dad round the track on a school day that put an hour's driving session on for the celebs to practice. As I was already instructing when I wasn't racing, this was fine. But it did take me a bit longer to get him to the same standard of driving round a track than was normal. He didn't seem to understand that the first corner after the start line was a corner you really needed to brake for.

It was a strange one and very challenging when going at speed into it. But dad nearly threw it off the track a couple of times, as I sprang into action to help on the steering wheel to control the car again.

I said to him "Dad, you really need to brake for Paddock hill bend, otherwise when you're on your own, you're going to go right off the track, and hopefully only get stuck in the gravel trap, if you don't brake going in fast, you are going to hit the barrier or even possibly roll first... so please brake when I tell you to."

"But Scotty, I need to feel when the car is going to do that to put the brakes on!" was his interesting reply.

"Dad, by the time you think it's time to brake with that thinking, it is already too late. You need to brake so you can get the front of the car to do what you want. With no brakes you're going to start to understeer off, then you'll lift off the power, the car's nose will dip and whichever direction you have the wheels pointing, the car is going to go... and its end of race!"

To be honest, it was great fun teaching him, but hugely difficult at the same time. Teaching family and bosses of businesses that are not used to being told what to do, are the hardest pupils. Here was a man who was both.

By the time race day came, I was confident he'd get around without hurting himself. Which was just want he needed. He was a competitive man, but not with mechanical things. For his race, it rained... Oh shit! I hadn't prepared him for this. Well it was wet, and slowly would dry, but still this was going to shake him.

At the start he got away slowly thanks to getting wheel spin on the wet track, but he managed to get through a very wet first corner, round the hairpin bend, then slightly slide off the track at the next bend. From the back of the pits you could be at the fence to see them coming. He got back on the track, and I could see into his car, and saw his eyes wide open and looking like they were on stalks. It was a ten-lap race, and after 5 long laps he came in for his swap over with Paul... Dad nearly didn't stop in the right place, they swapped over, and dad was relieved to get out, I think. He stumbled over to the garage where I was staying out of the way, caught sight of me, and gave his big grin as he came over, and put his arm around my neck.

"How did I do?" the relief really coming out now as he spoke.

"Well, 9th place dad, didn't you look at your pit board every lap?"

"What pit board?" was his reply that I was expecting anyway. Paul went on to drag their car up to 6th place by the end, which was good considering the field of novices at first before the handover to pro's had stretched the field out. It made for good watching as the real race drivers got on with the job of chasing each other for charity.

From this experience, Dad got an idea of what I did, and he was quite complimentary about it, asking questions like, "How do you keep that level of concentration up?" or "Is it always this tiring?" It was nice to have him get a glimpse of my world and realise that there was maybe more to it than just sitting down.

Dad was getting itchy feet again, New York was going well, London always riding high with the well to do and celebrities of the day. And the Hippodrome was a mecca for many people with bands and even circus acts for a while. But he wanted to spread his wings again, this time his focus went to Florida, and he wanted a club in Miami.

By this time, I had moved back down to London, as my mum had decorated the house since dad had left, and I was given the enormous front lounge that became my bedroom. I slipped back into visiting the clubs few times when the season was over and helping out at the club, too, on occasion.

I think I was still getting over the accident but kept that very much to myself. My results had improved, but only after a particular test day at Thruxton where I had inadvertently been lifting my foot off the throttle on corners that were easy flat out, which was my brain getting in the way.

I forced myself to enter the notorious flat-out corner called "Church" and put my left foot on my right foot on the throttle and pressed as hard as I could to break through my mental barrier. It worked, thank goodness, as it would have been a huge accident had it gone wrong.

For 1989 we had one last push for winning the Class B F3 championship. Dad was ok with that, even more so that Jim was still only asking for £90, 000 for the season, just like both the other seasons. Yet again Dad reminded me that for the money we had been spending, I could have a really nice flat in London, a Porsche and a bigger future with the clubs. But my heart was racetrack shaped. I was very happy racing cars, and I felt I could win the championship this time.

Yet again we had a launch at the club, we tried to do a video of the new car from a test day at Oulton Park, but our stupid video guys went to Alton Towers theme park first. So they were late, then while I did a warm-up lap on a chilly track, I had a minor off and damaged the front wings.

As we hadn't brought spares for what was only meant to be a video shoot, I had to dash back to get the spare, only to find on my return that the film crew couldn't wait and decide to get my six-foot-two mechanic with my helmet on to drive slowly for a lap or two with them following behind.

It was a complete cock up, and one my dad wasn't happy about, and neither was I. As far as I was concerned it was money wasted. But some of the footage was used, and just showed me how unprofessional the film crew were. Dad wasn't so bothered on the night; he was quite happy to let it go. And I think it was another one of those moments where dad and I were not on the same page, which told me more about him than he learned about me.

Dads plans for America were starting to take shape, and I didn't know it, but he was about to not just spread his wings, but fit jet engines to them, too. He was negotiating the sale of the Hippodrome and building the Miami to completion. He was also looking at a possible plot in Los Angeles, California.

Dad told me to be ready to change the livery on the car. I never pushed for Stringfellows on the car, even though in the early days I found it hard enough with the Hippodrome splashed all over everything. But to have Strings on the car still wasn't in my head. I honestly thought he had started another venture. So, I was intrigued to say the least, but forgot about it soon after. Like any good business entrepreneur, he had lots of ideas, but not all were followed up on. The car yet again looked great, and I hit the ground running. Dad nearly made it to the first race of the year, but he had to get back to America, which was a shame as I had qualified second for my class.

I stalled at the start, I got going again and then proceeded to climb back up the field. It was actually a blessing to miss the mad dash into the first series of corners at the first race of the year, so in a strange way, it helped me, though gave me a lot of work right up to the last lap. I managed to reclaim my 2nd position. A great race, but one I feel I should have won.

I was finishing on the podium on every outing, though not quite a win, which was frustrating. In the middle of the year, it's the British Grand Prix at Silverstone, and yet again British Formula 3 was one of the Support races. In fact, we were the race before the main event. Dad decided to use that event to unveil the car in its new livery, yes it was still a black car, but this time it had "Stringfellows" on it. And on the side pods, it said "London-New York-Miami". Not only that but a large marquee was organised for guests to enjoy with a meal and drink, with a disco for the evening planned.

It all looked great, and dad came over to the paddock before the start of the race with a few guests and a page 3 girl for photos. Having Debbie Ashby posing with you for pictures was very nice. And I still have the photos. I really should have got my shit together and asked her out. But my head was full of racing cars. I wasn't seeing anyone, but I did have my eye on someone, though I wasn't doing anything about making a move, at least not that weekend.

The race before a Grand Prix was always a good place to be as all the fans were staking their claim for a good viewing space, and the grandstands were virtually full because they want to be settled in plenty of time for the main event, however, formula 3 was good to watch because this was where some future F1 stars were and maybe even a future world champion.

I made a good start and being Silverstone, the circuit on the GP track is very wide in parts, but halfway around the first lap a Japanese driver in a Class A car decided, for no real reason, to bang wheels with me.

That was fine, plenty of room out of club corner, and I kept my foot in, right round until the chicane in front of a packed grandstand. When I braked for the chicane my car darted off to the right, and I went straight into the barrier. As I got out, I realised the front right wheel was punctured. It turned out that the guy who banged wheels with me had taken my tire valve out, so by the time I got to the chicane, the tire had no air in it.

I was gutted, not only out of the race on the first lap but right in front of all my guests and dad, as their watching position was perfectly in line with them on the opposite side of the track. The marshals came out when the coast was clear and pulled the car close up tight against the barrier.

By the time I got back to the hospitality tent, I was not feeling good at all. As I walked in, there was a cheer, and all my friends and guests stood and clapped. Somehow that made it all feel a little worse. But dad came over to me, and gave me a hug and said, "don't worry about it, Scotty, the car was perfectly placed for the cameras, I'm just pleased you're ok."

It was the best thing he could ever have said. In his eyes, it was good advertising because it was seen virtually every lap, and he saw I was ok. Anyway, there was a fun party to have now. This turned into dad and I on the mics stoking up the guests and dancing to great music.

Ironically that night we were the only Stringfellows open, as the London club had a water leak that closed the club for the night. That made the travelling Stringfellows show from Silverstone the most exclusive club in the country operational, with free entry and free drink! Crazy!

After that, I got my skates on and had a few more near wins, and an unfortunate non-finish at my beloved Oulton Park. That handed the championship to my rival Fernando Plata. However, I did get a win at Donnington, and again dad wasn't there for it. I won by a huge 25 seconds too. I gave my dad's Mum and Dad the trophy, which I have never seen since. I often wonder what happened to that.

My last race at Brands Hatch was a success by winning the Class B section of the F3 Super Prix, but as it was a depleted grid because budgets for some of the other class B teams were too tight for a non-championship race. When the race was over, I got out of the car in *parc fermé* and walked away without looking back. Doing that has stuck in my mind ever since, I'm not overly superstitious, but sometimes wonder if certain actions create a shift of direction in our fate.

Mine was to be brought into stark reality about life about three weeks later. I was seriously looking at moving away from Jim Lee to have a go at class A F3 for the next year. I wanted to go talk to West Surrey Racing, but they signed up Mika Häkkinen, and I knew that meant they would be concentrating on him. We all knew that if he got a better team and car, he would be winning a lot. So, I spoke to Alan Docking Racing, and if I could get £300,000 together, I would be fighting the front, and be in with a good shout for the championship.

Wow! £300K. I organised a meeting with Dad to set out my grand plan. But before I could even get around to the benefits of signing up with a front running team and a massive hike in budget. Dad had news for me.

"Scott, I'm afraid we can't sponsor you anymore. Not only are we still in the early days of the Miami club, which is developing slowly, but also, I'm going to be building a club in Los Angeles, in Beverly Hills no less. The sale of the Hippodrome doesn't cover it all. I need all the finance I can pull together for it. I'm sure you understand, Scotty, and I am sorry we can't do more, because you were doing so well this year too, which I am very pleased for you about."

This wasn't what I wanted to hear, but I suppose the warning signs were all there. And I didn't do what I should have been doing all year, which was to introduce potential new sponsors to my world and see my potential. It was my own fault for sitting back and not following up on other avenues for sponsorship, I just got comfortable thinking dad could do anything. I'm sure I wasn't the first or the last to be taken in by how easy how life was with a successful parent for a sponsor.

So, I had to let Alan Docking know, as well as Jim, that my racing had come to an abrupt halt.

But there was one good thing before the year was out. My mechanic Steve and I went to Florida to go stay at my Dad's place which was in a condominium on the coast, not far from Miami itself. On the first night dad took us to the club in Coconut Grove.

When we were ready my young friend, who was dressed up in his best going out clobber, was met with a quizzical look from my dad. "Steve, do you have any other suits with you" he enquired.

"No Peter, this is my best gear."

Dad looked him up and down and said. "Hmmm. You better come with me." Dad lead him to his walk-in wardrobe, where he proceeded to move suits around on the racks.

"Here try this on." Dad handed over a deep purple suit with big shoulders. My friend tried it on, and it just about fit. Well it looked better than the Manchester youth club suit he had.

"You look a hundred times better Steve. In fact, you can have that suit, it's not really my thing anyway," said dad, handing him the hanger for it.

I took a look at the label. "Bloody hell Steve, you better look after that. It's Jean Paul Gaultier Design suit."

He looked puzzled, "Is that good?"

"Good? If you're ever hard up for cash, sell this, and you'll be alright for a while that's for sure, Gaultier doesn't do mass-produced clothes, this is probably worth a couple of grand now!"

He promised he would look after it.

9

THE TRANSATLANTIC FAMILY

1990 was the start of a new decade, and I was without a drive. I wasn't instructing because I'd had an accident at Oulton Park at the beginning of 1989 and lost my job. This was a good thing in one way, because it made me concentrate on the great year ahead. But now I was without a drive, no work, and had just moved out of central London with my mum, who had just been zipping to and from America herself to visit friends in Los Angeles. Ironically. Dad was living half his life in the sky as it was with the clubs in New York, Miami and London. Add to that he was about to get an LA club up and running.

I did very little that year except go to my mother's wedding to the new man in her life after only knowing him a few months. My mum's wedding in Rutland, Vermont over in the States was really good, but I was still out of sorts.

This first year of a new decade was a time I started a decline. All my family were in America, my mum was in the throes of moving to LA, my sister Karen was travelling the world with her boyfriend, and Dad was flitting between London, New York and Miami, with the odd trip to LA trying to find the right place for another club. He was also still having meetings here there and everywhere to keep things going. It was about this time a friend of his took him to a lap dance club in Miami.

He wasn't interested at first, and was virtually dragged in, but instead of seeing a seedy club, he was shown a very glitzy club with a beautiful girl dancing on a pole. Also, many women in evening dresses filled the bar area. And after a few hours and several hundred dollars later, with nothing but a virtually naked woman dancing really close to him to show for it, a light bulb moment hit him. His friend got him in touch with the guy who was behind all this, and some ideas were thrown around.

I managed to get a race in. I yet again used my own money, which wasn't a lot. It was in a Class A car at Silverstone. About a week before the race I did an outdoor charity Kart race, and while pratting around in the back of my friend's car on the way home which was full of people, he threw the car into a fast bend on the road. I was thrown across the back where I tried to brace myself but felt a terrific pain as I did right in my chest.

I thought I was having a heart attack. But I'd seriously strained one of my chest muscles. It was a tough week leading up to the race as I raced against time to get better, in hindsight I should have cancelled, and tried to do race later in the year. But I was impetuous and stupid. I didn't do well.

In December 1990 dad was opening the Beverly Hills club, and I was to go over for the opening. I went a couple of days early and dad showed me round. It was amazing, and to this day I still think it was the best club he ever built. It had a bar and restaurant and a piano stage downstairs, and the disco upstairs.

Best of all we were situated at the top of a hill that had been specially made to look like a street in Europe. It looked very Italian influenced to me. It was a great setting, and shops would move into the other properties over time as the street developed. Then dad asked me if I could be lighting DJ as the one he was expecting wasn't going to make it for the opening.

Sure, I'd love to do that, this was the latest equipment he had, and I was shown the rig by a clearly fast-thinking, annoying, high IQ type American, who spoke at a hundred miles an hour and expected me to think like him.

It took me a couple of goes to get him to slow down and realise he was annoyed that I wanted to work it my way, more manual than using all the flashing scenarios he'd programmed into the computer. He didn't seem to get that flashing the lights to the beat of the music and sometimes certain colours were an integral part of making the lights dance to the music, not just random flashes. We didn't hit it off.

But I did the opening, and all went well, so well that for a trip was only meant to be for 10 days, I stayed for a month! I was paid back at home, so that got around any working laws as I didn't have a green card, the name of the permit to live and work in America.

Dad had put me up in an iconic hotel up the road. The Rodeo Drive Hotel was just a stone throw away from the club and walking to work or home from it was amazing as I always felt safe, even at 4:30 and being at a diner with some of the staff afterword.

Beverly Hills had its own police, and they were always on corners and cruising the streets. I also splashed out a bit on my hire car, I used a Ford Mustang Mach1 convertible, but better than that, it was from "Rent-a-Wreck!"

It was scratched to buggery inside and out, but I loved it, and the convertible roof never went up while I had it. It was brilliant. But after ten days at fifty-five dollars a day, I had to change it, as I couldn't afford that for longer. So, I got a VW Golf or Rabbit as they called it, for fourteen dollars a day.

On one of the nights in the club dad called me over to the bar area where he was with some people, whom at the time had their backs to me. I moved past them and turned around to see Rod Stewart and Rachel Hunter in front of me. Dad said "Rod, you remember my son, don't you? last time you saw him you bounced him on your knee" I think this surprised both Rod and I at the same time

"Bloody hell peter you know how to make an old friend feel really old. Hello Scott, nice to meet you," was Rod's almost stunned surprise as in front of him me, now a lad of 24 years old.

"Hello Rod, nice to meet you... again, I guess!" We both had a laugh and shook hands. He was to get married to Rachel about a week later, and my dad went to the wedding with Frizzby.

  I had a great time while there and made a few friends and had a bit of time with a rather nice crazy redhead too. I stayed long enough to celebrate Christmas and New Year's in America. Then I headed back home in time for my birthday.

Being back in England after all that excitement was like coming down to earth with a bump. But my determination to get back behind the wheel on a track was stronger than ever. I still wasn't ready to get back involved with the club life, not yet anyway. But I had considered it while out in LA. I was taken by the high life I was on the edge of, but the northern racer within was too strong. I did often wonder how life would have been if I'd settled in LA. It was some kind of irony that for a country that I loved going to, the rest of my family had ended up living over there for a time. Karen came back from her round the world trip and settled in New York. First, she worked for dad before forming her own design company with her future husband Paul.

Pretty soon I was the only Stringfellow living in his country of birth. But 1991 was a time of gritting my teeth and getting on with it. I used some of my own money and somehow got a drive for what was going to be six races in the British Saloon car championship, in a Ford Cosworth Sapphire.

The car looked great: the team was called Maxted Motorsport. I was going to dabble in saloon car racing for the first time, well since my Brands Hatch school days races. My racing was to start some way into the championship as it was well on its way already.

I was going to learn. Though I was a single-seater racer at heart, at least this car was rear-wheel drive, which was the same as everything else I'd driven to this point. I told Dad about it, and I think he was genuinely pleased I was getting out of single-seaters, as he told me much later on, he thought they looked way too fast and dangerous. Parents.... what can you do?

About a week or so before my first test day, I went to Oulton Park to see my mate Richard testing in preparation for his 5th British F3000 race of the year. And I also went to talk to some of the other drivers who I knew who was doing it. Paul Warwick was also a close friend, not quite as close as Richard, but Paul and I got on well, and he had visited the club a few times. I had also made him a member of the club too.

He seemed shy, but he had a great sense of humour and was a bloody quick driver since he found the F3000 more to his liking and had won the first four races already that year. So, I was at the testing on the Friday, but I didn't stay for qualifying or the race, I had something else to do on the Sunday.

By Sunday night I was home when I got a phone call. I can't remember who told me now, maybe my latest crap manager, but the news wasn't good. Paul had lost his life while leading the race with my mate Richard behind him. Paul's car had suddenly turned sharp left at the notorious Knickerbrook corner.

It hit the tire wall so hard it broke the car and threw Paul over the fence and onto the banking where spectators were. I couldn't believe it. Richard told me much later that for about 15 minutes after the accident he'd given up racing, because he had stopped to help at the scene of what was clearly a big one and looked up and saw where Paul had landed and how still he was. He knew it was over.

There was much shedding of tears by everyone I knew once it was confirmed he had passed away. Crazy as it may sound, another friend of mine had been killed only the week before at the same corner, but for an even more freaky reason. The guy had pierced his brain stem with a poorly fitted headrest after hitting the wall front first. For Paul it was the ferocity of hitting the tire wall after a front damper snapped under load into the corner. There was nothing he could have done.

I was devastated, and when I told my Dad, he was philosophical, sad, and probably very pleased it wasn't me racing that day. He had met Paul and had seen how shy he was in the club, but Paul opened up more the better you knew him. A week later I was to test my new race car at Brands Hatch, the same day of the funeral, which wasn't far away from the track.

I don't know why, but I decided to do the test, then at the lunch break go to the funeral, and then go back to Brands to do more testing. What was I thinking?

I tested in the morning, had a great time and got near the lap record. Stopped and went to the funeral. It was the most sobering thing I'd seen since the last racer's funeral I attended in 1986. The number of people and flower wreaths was astonishing. I was one of the people that threw dirt into the hole where the coffin lay. I was in the line next to Dave Coyne, who was also in the same race and saw the whole thing.

Afterwards, I went to the local pub with Richard, Dave and most of the drivers I knew at the time. We drank with the Warwick family, and was told that amongst the things they put in the coffin, they also put his Stringfellows membership card. That choked me up, and my dad was quite speechless when I told him about it later.

I went back to Brands, got in the car and couldn't concentrate, I was nowhere near the pace I had been in the morning, and I pulled into the pits and didn't want to do the rest of the day, my heart just wasn't in it. I think it was seeing his helmet laid on the top of the coffin and throwing the dirt in that played on my mind.

I went home and called my dad up. He was very good and didn't ask me if I was going to stop racing or anything. He just listened and was really good. It hadn't stopped me wanting to race, but it had given me pause for thought.

Top: Dad and I in1989 After the disastrous British Grand Prix support race. Dad assures me everything is ok.

Middle: Dad and I posing for cameras in the Silverstone Paddock. The first race we ran with Stringfellows on the car.

Bottom: Me in the Stringfellows car,1989 British Formula 3 waiting to go on to the track to qualify.

Top: My dad's Corvette Sting-ray in 1978, the first car I ever drove.

Middle: Dad, my sister Karen and I in the club.

Bottom: My 30th birthday party at String-fellows 1996.

Top: 1986 BRSCC Awards night. Mum and Dad saw me collect my FF1600 Champion of Oulton trophy, one of two championships I won that year.

Bottom: 2017 A quick snap of Dad and I while at Palma Airport in Mallorca while we wait for our plane home.

10

CARS IN LONDON & AMERICA

When we moved to London, Dad had a Cream Mercedes Benz 350SL, and my mum a Gold Triumph TR7 and by this time my sister had a VW Golf GTi Convertible in white. We got to move to a new house after a year in Islington north London and on to Marylebone Road.

We didn't have a garage, but we had a courtyard that we shared with other residents. Dad gave my mum his Mercedes, and he got a lovely black Rolls-Royce Corniche convertible. This was very much his style, with lovely cream interior too.

The King of Clubs should have a very nice car, it is a status symbol, and the 80's were full of those. When he lost his licence for drink driving, he gave the car away to charity. He then took on a chauffeur who had his own car. Which gave him freedom to drink. But after about four years, and he'd only lost his licence for two years, he got back into the idea of driving. He kept it a secret of what car he was going to get and wound me up for days as I was guessing all the flash stuff.

On the day I was watching out of the window of our apartment, because he said I would know it when I saw it. And I did... a bright pink Fiat Gamine Vignale homed into view. I can't say I was impressed, knowing dad though it made sense. There wouldn't be another on the road in London, and it stood out. He liked to have a spotlight on him, and this was perfect.

It looked stupid to me, and it was a 1958 car. The technology didn't exist then what he had been used to. This thing had no power steering, a non-synchromesh gearbox and no disk brakes. I drove it and knew he wouldn't stick this for long. It was a summer fun car in truth, and he didn't have the garage to tuck it away in. I thought he would get rid of it after a few months, but he stuck it out for nearly a year, only because he kept taking my mum's car when the weather was bad or just too cold.

When he moved out, he got a VW beetle convertible in black, a nice car that got stolen. He then went in for a BMW 530i. Which was also black, but with blacked-out windows. I borrowed it for a week once while I was between cars after my VW Golf GTi had blown a valve out of the engine at a racetrack while I was using it for instructing work. Honestly moving about in a black BMW with blacked-out windows made me look like a pimp! And dad later on even asked if I wanted to take it on when he wanted to change cars again, but the fuel economy was terrible, so he gave it to his brother Geoff.

Once dad got firmly into America, he had a car in every city he had a club at, and a house or apartment. His choice of car was a Jeep. He had one in New York, a nice black one, and he had one in Miami, a white one. Like his old Jeep from years ago, that had a huge golden eagle sticker on the bonnet, both cars had the club emblem of the butterfly on their bonnets. In LA he just hired a convertible anything whenever he went over.

Back at home, he seemed to lose interest in cars for a while, and even for a short while until he got another car after losing the Beetle, he borrowed my car, which was a Peugeot 306 Turbo D back then, as I had just got a Honda Integra Type-R but not let go of the Pug. He liked that.

When he got a new place in London, he got an electric car, which was a good idea, except he got a rubbish one. It was an Italian thing called a Maranello, not Ferrari connected but very small, plasticky and it was awful. After that, he ended up getting another electric car, but this time a Smart car, the ones made by Mercedes. He also got a Porsche again, a 911 Carrera 4S convertible, and I loved it. I got to borrow it a few times until he sold it and got a Range Rover Evoque, and then followed that with a Jaguar XE 3.0 R-Sport, which was a great car, and the last one he would have.

Back to the '90s

Apart from the tragedy of losing two friends in 1991, the year went pretty well, I got into racing the saloons, but Dad was too busy to come to a race. So, I did three British rounds, and then blew the rest of my budget on doing the Spa-Francorchamps 24 hours race in Belgium.

That was brilliant, and one I would love for dad to have come to see. But things were warming up in America. He was really spinning plates as my mum would put it. The clubs in the states were occupying all his time, and he was on and off trans-Atlantic flights so often, I think his air miles would have reached the moon and possibly back.

During this period of time I didn't see any of my family at all, and I was living alone in Enfield, Middlesex. Dad was away fighting battles I had no clue about. The America experience was proving to be a difficult one, but like any good duck dad looked all calm on the surface. Underneath that calm and together man was another man pedalling away like crazy to keep the show going and looking as it should.

Despite that, things sometimes looked strange. For a long while I was worrying that maybe my dad was drinking too much, as on occasion in London he would be seen being led out of the club buy one of the staff back to his apartment, which was now next door, so it wasn't far for him to go.

Miami was developing, but way too slowly to be comfortable, the location at the time wasn't right, as beautiful as it was, but as he wasn't right on a beach or in central Miami. Even though at some point the TV show "Only fools and horses" did a special show that used the club in one of its episodes. That was pretty good kudos, but not enough to change things for him.

New York was struggling too, and then LA was just not making the money he expected because everyone seemed to be famous for something or was a friend of someone famous and just didn't want to pay their way. LA was a huge disappointment for Dad, as he wanted the stars to come in and play hard, while others came to be part of that. But dad soon learned that the stars were very aware that they were possibly being watched and reputation was everything. Poor or outrageous behaviour was pounced on and suing one another a virtual national pastime.

Dad worked out that the stars took their craziness home and did it there out of the sight of prying eyes, unless you needed to be seen at the trendiest restaurant in town at that time, where being able to get a table at the drop of a hat rather than book weeks in advance was a measure of your power, and power in America was the real currency.

I worked out I was in mourning for a loss of momentum with my career in motorsport. Any manager I got never could get anything moving or close up any deals as the stigma of being the son of a social celebrity wasn't what sponsors wanted. You'd think I would be well placed in getting a good sponsor, but there was another problem. The sponsor just wanted to get close to my dad for endorsements for them by him.

I even got close to a deal with a big speaker manufacturer, but it soon dawned on me that they really wanted him, not me. This made me withdraw a lot, I ended up not going out except to get food, I was completely at a loss.

As 1992 rolled round I was heading very downhill, I drank but not a lot. I just reverted into myself. Dad was full onto a new direction. He had taken a full run at New York after closing it down for a short while and refurbishing the place. He got into a partnership with another club owner who had lap dancing clubs called "Pure Platinum" and pretty soon the club was reopened and renamed "Stringfellows presents Pure Platinum" and rebranded as an all-girl cabaret club. Dad hated the term "lap dance" or "strip club". Strippers to him were a seedy name with the wrong stigma attached. This was a girl club with beautiful girls/ladies dancing up close. He eventually changed it to something far classier. A "Gentleman's Club."

I was still trying to go racing again, but not instructing... it was a personal battle. I was slipping into depression. If you've had it or know someone who has suffered, it's an illness, an illness with no outward signs except for in extreme cases, poor self-hygiene. I wasn't that bad, but I was struggling to find a way out of my self-disillusionment. It's the lack of self-determination that seemed to consume me, I could feel myself being pulled down.

I was alone in Enfield, no girlfriend, no pets, no get-up-and-go. Eating was beginning to feel like a waste of time and effort, and I was making myself ill. The house was paid for, I was lucky beyond by having my bills paid by my mum. I was in the best position ever to get something going, but I was down and out. At least I had a roof over my head. I look back on all that now and wish I was able to go back in time and shake the fuck out of myself to stop being a hermit, and grow some balls to knock on doors, get my life going while I had the golden opportunity of having no responsibilities!

But depression closes the eyes and ears, and it needs someone to notice outside of yourself to help you through. A chink of light within myself realised I needed help, and this only came about because I'd visited a "Toys R Us" store to buy a jigsaw to pass the time, but I was wearing ragged jeans and a t-shirt, and I looked awful as I had not shaved for a few days.

Honestly, I looked a mess, but I only realised how bad I must have looked when I realised I was being shadowed by the store security guy. It was a small wake up call, so I grabbed one of those large 1000-piece jigsaws and got out of the shop. It made me feel very embarrassed.

When I got home, I looked at the picture on the box properly, it was like a sign or something, a subconscious shout from within I guess, if you believe in that sort of thing. The picture was of the New York skyline from the docks. It made me do something, it made me ask for help, and I called both my mum and Dad, who both were living in America at the time, Dad in New York, and my mum in South Carolina in a tiny town called McCormick. She had a huge house in 83 acres of land just outside of it.

It was decided that I would go spend a couple of weeks in New York and then mum and her husband would drive up and pick me up to take me back to South Carolina. They were going further north to Rutland in Vermont anyway, so they would pick me up on their way back while passing through. That sounded like a great idea and picked me up quite a bit. At least I had plans now rather than nothing but watching TV and playing on my video games.

11

CRAZY TIMES ACROSS THE POND

Getting on a long-haul flight for me is always a wonderful time, but this time I was in some sort of glassy daze. My emotions were constantly just under the surface, and I was doing Oscar nomination performances of holding it together.

Again, depression fights you in your mind and tries to keep you down. But my inner self saw the light at the end of the tunnel, even though my depression was putting fears in my thoughts. What if I miss a chance to race again? A sponsor might be asking for me, and I was out of the country? In reality none of this was happening or likely to happen, I was out of the loop in the racing circle.

Once the plane got above the clouds, and I had a Martini and lemonade in my hand, I was relaxing, looking out at the clouds below with the sun shining from above the aircraft. Unlike some people, I felt safe. The hum of the engines and the feeling of being away from my problems was almost Zen-like, even now I really love that moment on a plane.

Once in New York, I got a cab and went to the hotel dad had put me in. The New York Hilton was an imposing sight, and that's a good trick in a city that is nothing but stupidly tall buildings.

I was shown to my room which I remember was on the 43rd floor, the highest I've ever been in a hotel room. It was a lovely sunny day, and I was in New York, the city that never sleeps. But I was going to get some jetlag I was sure of that, so I needed to stay awake as long as possible to get into the hours. Later Dad came to meet me at the hotel, and we went to the club together.

It was the first time I'd been to the club since the refit, and the last time it was the opening in 1986, so dad had been trying to conquer America for seven years. And here he was, still trying to get a foothold. Little did I know how tough it was for him, and he had been quietly trying to get out of America for the last two years. Then this last opportunity to make it came around, he changed the design of the club enough to accommodate the dancing poles, and really ramped up the opulence that other clubs would have to raise their game to reach. In our fabulous restaurant I ate with dad as over on the poles I could see girls dancing in long dresses.

The real game was about paying for the girl of your choice to come dance at your table up close, but with no touching. I was very innocent, young but old enough to be in there. After our meal dad called over two ladies, and they proceeded to dance close up to me, both at the same time. My dad sat nearby. That was freaky to me, I didn't know where to look once the dress was off. At this stage in the business knickers and shoes stayed on, but the dancing was close.

They were both very nice, and my dad got a kick out of watching me squirm a little. Once the song they were dancing to changed, they stopped, lent forward and both kissed me on each of my cheeks. Dad then said, "Okay, Scotty pay the ladies!"

"Err... with what?" was my withering reply. At which point Dad laughed and threw what was $200 worth of what I was to learn was known as heavenly dollars. I nearly gave it all to them both, but dad said "it's up to you, but its only $20 a dance..." So, I gave them $20 each and... saved the rest, for later perhaps. I was catching on very fast.

Eventually, dad told me to go sit by the stage with the girls while he got on with checking the club out and talk to some customers he knew. The two stunning giggling girls took me to the stage and introduced me to American style drinking. When the waitress came over to take our order, I asked for a Martini and Lemonade.

One of the girls said, "Oh no, you can't drink that here baby, this is New York. You need a JD straight, on the rocks!"

I was happy to try something new, so I said "Okay," And that was my first introduction to Whiskey, or more accurately Jack Daniels Bourbon whiskey on a couple cubes of ice. And for my gentle palate it was strong. Lucky for me, I didn't drink much, but it did help me sleep. And no, I didn't wake up with two women in my hotel bed.

The next day was another glorious day, and I made a sudden discovery. My depression was lifting. I didn't have a clue where to go, and New York is a very big city. But I found a diner a couple of streets away that wasn't only a little famous, but I'd also been to its sister restaurant in LA, The Carnegie Diner. I also found a more well-known diner, thanks in part to a song and a TV sitcom. Tom's Diner was the subject of a song by American singer Suzanne Vega and had a cameo role on the TV show Seinfeld. I took in the sights, like a visit to both the Empire State Building, and the twin towers, of which nobody would ever dream what was to happen to them in another nine years. From the viewing areas at each, New York was a spectacular place to see and be in.

Again, later in the evening dad took me on the town, this time to another club, which he had just taken over. He really was on a roll in the land of the mighty Dollar, it was called "El Morocco," and it was not so far away from the other club.

He didn't make any changes except put poles in and the décor was already a theme, a kind of African zebra print on the furniture and some walls. I quite liked it, it was smaller than Strings but had a nice warm and inviting feel to it too. Also, I got to know a waitress there.

In fact, we got together a lot and for the two weeks I stayed in NY I spent a lot of it with her. My depression was giving way to a late development of "wild child" like mentality, or just I was becoming like my dad! But at 26 years old with no ties, I was relaxing a lot after the few years of no proper racing and fretting about it constantly.

After the two weeks were up, it was time to move on. I'd had a lot of fun and spent more time with my dad than I had for years. The clubs looked great, despite whatever was going on behind the scenes, he put on a good show.

I was picked up by my mum, and a 14-hour drive to McCormick South Carolina was made. My time in New York went a long way to sort out my depression. The craziness didn't end there, as while I spent the next two months with my mum and her husband, I met another woman, who was a friend of my sister's from the days when she lived in NY too.

This lady had her own business and was very attractive, and I nearly got married to her! All in the space of 2 months! But I woke up and realised it wasn't going to work with her, and she agreed. We are still friends to this day, but only via Facebook. At the time though, I was clutching at straws because I'd lost direction. I had been talking on the phone with dad a fair few times, which he was quite instrumental in talking me down out of my crazy phase.

Back to Life

I got back to England and managed to do something about the racing.

I did two races at Donington Park in the Formula Vauxhall Lotus championship. But I didn't have a great time, though

I had joined up with Jim Lee Racing again for it, but now he was called Team JLR. My engine had a problem, and promptly broke. It was found out later to be a manufacturing fault, not mine! Again, this event had come out of my own pocket, but nothing came of it, which was a shame.

I slipped back into my old ways again. But this time I was throwing a sponsor proposal together, instead of wasting my time, apart from visiting the club from time to time with friends.

The next few years changed a little, as I got back into instructing and I even raced a little. I managed to get regular instructing work for some racing schools and manufacturer days, which lead onto my being able to get dad involved in a few things on track.

I was going to do a track day and drive different cars with dad along to have a go too. I was going to write about it for a magazine. It was great fun. We went to Thruxton circuit in Hampshire, a track I had grown to love. We drove a few cars and had a great laugh.

But when I took him for a run in a Porsche 911 with twin turbos and a boost tap in the car, I realised Dad wouldn't be able to cope with this one, and I told him so. As I accelerated out of a long sweeping bend towards the corner called Church, I felt wheelspin while being in 4th gear, it was that moment I said to dad "Sorry, but I don't think you should drive this one, Dad"

"Oh yeah, why's that?' he yelled back over the sound of this beast of a car."

"Because we are at 120 now and it's wheel spinning. If you back off mid corner in this, you won't catch it. Just lifting off the power will be like hitting the brakes" I yelled back.

I looked across at dad in the passenger seat. His eyes were very wide! I turned into the corner and kept a steady power on as the rear end drifted out. It was a lovely feeling to me, but I think my dad was holding his breath. He did drive everything else that day though. It was a good job I drove us home, as per usual, he was head back mouth open and asleep all the way home.

Back in the USA dad's American dream was coming to an end, and he was pulling back to England. The LA club shut down because the landlords wouldn't drop the rent for a year, which may have saved it. He had no plans to make that a girl club. It was way too good as it was.

Miami closed because it just wasn't pulling in the crowds. It was just too far away from Miami central to attract more attention, and its location was developing too slowly, ironically that area now is a hive of activity. He was just too far ahead of his time for that one. New York was going well, but the people he was partnered with were causing problems, and he needed to take this concept to London where he felt safe.

He got into bringing the Gentleman's Club to Great Britain in his own club in London. This meant a lot of court appearances for new licence agreements, and a steady change from internationally acclaimed disco fame to gentleman's club.

Meanwhile, I was getting my head more into race instructing and getting myself into working at more tracks. Both of us were climbing our own personal mountains, but dad's mountain was very different from mine. He was immensely brave in his quest, but he was spurred on by the fact that the New York club had made a massive profit in its first year after the makeover and change in direction, which my dad wanted to repeat in London.

Though the disco wasn't doing bad, he could see the financial implications of the girl club boosting that enormously, providing he could get the right people in...

At this time, I used to see dad sporadically, and sometimes he would have a full three-piece suit on, which I knew was his "court look". Being a personality in a courtroom wasn't the way to go, and he knew that. He respected the law, and already had a good relationship with the police in the area, which it has to be said took time to establish from the moment he arrived in London in 1980.

Dad took a dancer from New York into the courtroom and she explained her role. She explained it so well and calmly that getting the permission for the appropriate licenses went well. There are many you need for opening a club, depending on what you are serving, music playing hours and opening hours. There are hoops you must jump through. Dad followed them all up. He tackled everything.

He was good at courting the press too. He played the game, he wasn't afraid of what they would write, because he understood they were just trying to keep their circulation large. Sensational headlines and half made up stories about celebs were just part of it. So, he never really made too much fuss over stuff about him.

But the media in general would go to him for all sorts of quotes, because he was approachable and always had an opinion that made good copy.

Television Man

He was also always getting approached for TV ideas and invited onto game shows. He went on "Blankety Blank" twice, once with Terry Wogan and also when Les Dawson presided over the show. He also went on "Never Mind the Buzzcocks", but they put him on the wrong side of the set which didn't help his deafness in one ear.

He also went on "Have I got News for You". The thing about that show is it's less about the game of winning points as more about looking at political or other news stories in a funny way, that and send up the new guest. Trouble is my dad genuinely read the papers every day, and he wanted to win. Strange how he didn't go on again.

There was TV shows that included him in on those type of shows that were about his era, 60's music and the odd one about other stars from the past. He was also in the audience for a series with some huge star, and the audience was full of TV stars and celebs themselves. On one such show it was the erratic comedian Freddie Star, and dad was dragged out of the audience for some magic trick, and Freddie proceeded to pretend... quite convincingly, to cut my dad's famous long hair. It was well done, and as dad said, you never knew if Freddie was going to do it for real or not.

At some point we were both in on a documentary type show called "Relative Values" and we were interviewed separately in our homes. But we also did a day at Donington Park racetrack, with me instructing Dad around the circuit with cameras onboard. It was the most fun I'd had with dad up to that point.

It took me longer, again, to teach dad the basics that it took me normally. But the bigger reason this time was that he was playing up to the cameras in the car, and outside and anyone watching on the pit lane wall. Also, he refused to take off his stupid mirrored dark sunglasses for ages, until I finally got him to take them off. Once he started to concentrate, he got better and better.

At the end of what felt almost like a grand prix distance, he became good. When we got back in the pit lane once I thought we had done enough, we came to a stop and for a moment when the car was switched off, he seemed to get what was so great about being on a track. He actually said he'd enjoyed that.

We did one more run on track, this time with me driving, and it was fast laps. I strapped him in tight, and away we went. He seemed to enjoy it, but I knew I was scaring the pants off him, which was great fun, and I have all of this on video! Priceless.

When the program came out, I got to see what he had to say about me. Quite frankly I was shocked, he seemed to see me as a racing driver who crashed a lot. He said I was childish about how I acted when my mum and he split up! It was like he didn't really know me at all. We were very different about many things, and I suppose the fact we occupied different worlds explained a lot. I knew more about his world than he knew about mine only because I was brought up in his world and he rarely occupied mine.

It was the first time I saw something else about my Dad. He could be supportive, but also hurt me with his words. I really don't think he knew what he was saying. He was just making the show more interesting in his own way but blinkered to how maybe it might affect me and my quest to find a sponsor for racing again. Sponsors don't want a crasher, or an emotional wreck!

12

CHANGING TRACK (IN MORE WAYS THAN ONE)

Onwards into an uncertain time, I was instructing a bit but wanting to move to a new house. Commuting on the M25 was driving me mad. By 1997 I was really looking hard, I found, like so many others, the closer you got to London the more expensive it was to buy. Anyway, I didn't want to get closer to London, I wanted to get away. I realised that most of my journeys were between Donington and Thruxton, which became the two main schools of racing I worked at.

So, it would make sense to live outside of the M25 and somewhere between the two. After a snoop round about 12 houses I found at my third different area, and 14th house where I wanted to be. It was a nice little house with a garden and a garage that had its own driveway connected to the nice little semi. I moved to Aylesbury in 1998. Dad was surprised and a bit critical at my being an hour out of London.

But that's how I liked it, and I didn't get to use the M25 again... unless it was a track day at Brands Hatch. Then it was only an hour and a bit to the track from my house. Once I moved in, I tried to get dad to visit, but he acted like driving an hour to my house was a monumental task. Who was being childish now?

Around this time dad was taking regular trips out to Ibiza in the Balearic Islands in the middle of the Mediterranean Sea.

He had got himself a Sunseeker speed boat, well, it was the kind of speed boat you could live in kind of. It was a 48-foot Superhawk as I think it was called. He found his hobby at last.

Well, he had a boat out in Florida years before, and trust me, he was much better driving a boat than any car. He had the control and understanding of his boat like I had with a racing car, only things happened a lot different on a boat. It always amazed me that on a boat he could concentrate, look ahead, and follow the sea rules.

This was his escape from thinking clubs. He didn't follow any sport or even play golf. He loved his boats. The one he had in Florida, in the days of the Miami club, I went on with him a couple of times, and one of those times he had to park it beside a fuel stop on fast-flowing river, between two other boats. The slot was just big enough, and he parked it with such skill, it was wonderful to watch.

While he was in Ibiza, most times with a girlfriend, he would go to night clubs and bars not far from the port where he was parked up and be relaxed with all the crazy people. He liked the clubs but wasn't like the druggy types that the rave clubs attracted. He was recognised by the Brits abroad, and always well treated.

He also got into going to Mallorca, to the point that eventually he would park the boat over in Port Portals on Mallorca Island and used that as his base. He didn't get a hotel because he would live out of his boat. I would fly into Mallorca sometimes on my own, sometimes also with a girlfriend.

And on one of those trips we, meaning dad and his lady together with me and my fun lady at the time went on his boat to Ibiza, it was only meant to be a day trip, but it was a bit of a trek between the two islands. It was great fun. I did a lot of steering too, following the course heading with the compass.

We were all having drinks, nothing heavy, and some food was prepped on the way. But with about half an hour to go I started feeling funny. Now I don't get seasick, but I quickly deduced it was something else that I'd started having trouble with, called Meniere's. It's a disease that comes and goes for a period of time. I started to lose balance on the boat, and I felt awful...

Dad knew exactly what it was, and just made sure I was laid flat, while he slowed the boat and kept it smooth all the way to Ibiza. When he was close enough, I could hear he was on his phone calling a friend to help and organise somewhere for me to stay. Once we arrived, I was well and truly dizzy and panicking slightly because I was sweating like crazy too. This was really uncomfortable in a hot country.

I was helped to a nearby apartment. I asked dad if I was going to end up in hospital, but he assured me it wasn't going to last forever. And he preceded to tell me that he himself had experienced this and had hoped it was going to skip a generation. See the old Stringfellow Keep-it-to-yourself ploy was in full swing.

It now made sense why I had sometimes seen dad being led out of the club looking like he was half cut. He wasn't drunk, he was just having a Meniere's attack. He just didn't let too many people in on the condition, and here was I having the same thing. He told me his lasted about five years, and the trips to Mallorca seemed to help.

I stayed in the apartment, with my new, but very pissed off, girlfriend just being nearby, and even went on a shopping trip for some food. Eventually, after about three hours, it wore off, but I felt knackered. Not wanting to ruin the trip I let dad know I was okay on my phone, but he said we were going to stay the night, and if I felt up to it, we would all go into the town of the port for a night out.

Our respective girlfriends got on great. We visited a few bars and dance clubs until Dad decided he wanted to go back to the boat, but his younger girlfriend wanted to stay out. Dad said ok and I'd look after them both. Which was nice, and all good until his girl decided she wanted to go back too, but by this time it was something like 1 a.m. and I said we would walk her back to the boat, whereupon my girlfriend said she wanted to stay.

Of course, I possibly should have suggested we all go together, but my dad's girl was already stalking off as she was quite pissed and very much of the instant nature kind of girl at the best of times. My girlfriend said not to worry about her and go, she would wait there. I didn't like that, the place was rammed with people, and I worried within that if something happened to her, I'd have no way of tracking her down. But off I went with the pissed one, who incidentally was a young actress, but also had the legs of a gazelle. When I stupidly suggested we jog to the boat, trying to cut the time away from my girl as crazy scenarios developed in my head, she was off, not jogging but running with consummate ease.

Now I was fairly fit thanks to my racing days, but I hated running. Just keeping up with this girl was like going for a run with Usain Bolt to me. And to add to that the boat was on the other side of the harbour and she was leading the way. Just as we got close to the boat, she started shouting "PE-TER...PETER... DARLING I'M HOME" Dad emerged from the inner cabin stark naked. Obviously, he didn't expect me to be with her, and it was bloody late. I was expecting him to roll out the walkway to the jetty, but he didn't have to, as lady gazelle literally leapt on board from the land once again showing the power of her very long shapely legs.

Meanwhile I was half bent over well out of breath, with enough strength to say to dad... "I thought I..... should escort her.... back..." Dad gave a little smile and said, "Thanks, Scotty".

My walk back was more a brisk walk, with bursts of a jog as my thoughts returned to my girl. When I made it back to the bar where the music was still pumping, and the place thronged with bodies dancing and drinking, she wasn't where I'd left her. I scanned the room and found her dancing along with a guy behind her who was holding her hands and dancing very close.

I wondered if I should just watch for a while and see how things were, but I realised that was a stupid attitude to have, and only leads to distrust. So, I did the next best thing. I circled round the back and came up behind them. I put my head in front and said "Hi, I'm back."

I noticed that she dropped his hands very quickly. I said, "I think we should go back to the apartment now as it has been a long day."

She agreed and turned to her "friend", she held out a hand and said thanks to looking after her. It was a strange, almost uncomfortable interaction. As we turned to leave, I thanked the guy too. But I know she must have got his number, or he had hers, I got the feeling she was that type of girl.

As we made our way back the evening air hit her, and she became the annoying kind of drunk that insists they know their way home, and to let them walk, or stagger in this case. She ended up following the right path, but followed the pattern in the pavement which was an ornate winding design, so it was quite funny to watch, but took a lot longer than it should and when we got back she wouldn't let me help her get undressed, and she fell off the end of the bed numerous times, before passing out. Two things crossed my mind while I got ready for bed.

One, funny how I had arrived like a drunk person with a dizzy head, and now here she was in much the same way but had to drink to get her into that state. And secondly, when we got back to England, I think this relationship would probably be over. The journey back after a nice breakfast in the port was uneventful, both girls were very quiet, but once back on the boat my dad's girl livened up a little more when we got closer to Mallorca again.

The boat was one of the few places my dad was himself again. You could see him visibly relax, I'm sure he still thought about the club. Every day the club was never far away, but he learnt how to keep it on one side while in Mallorca, and especially while on his boat. He had a lot of adventures on it.

A few years later he got another one, a bigger one. A Sunseeker again, but the Camargue 55 this time, which was about as big as you could go without a crew to man it. He loved it, and this one was easier to live on. Also, it had a spare bedroom... I say bedroom, but it was just a small area with two bunk beds within, nothing fancy. Unfortunately, I never got to stay over anywhere in, but I did grab a snooze once or twice on future trips.

I have since instructed in a few cars that would remind me of dad's pride and joy. The TVR cars are particularly good for that, the Tuscans and Chimeras are almost dead ringers for the boat if you closed your eyes, the sound of the engine and the smell of the leather seats... It's all there. I've not been in one since we lost dad. I dread, but at the same time, I'm intrigued to see how it would affect me when I do.

*I just remembered, I once nearly bought a TVR, one without power steering, it was lovely. But I chickened out because I didn't think I would be able to afford to run it. On fuel consumption alone, it would have crippled me financially, but it sure would have been nice to have. *

I got settled into my life of avoiding the M25. I worked at Donington, Thruxton and a bit at Bedford too for a purely corporate track day company. But I also travelled to other tracks too, Oulton Park, Cadwell Park, Snetterton and sometimes Brands Hatch, which did mean a trundle round the M25 circle of torture. My instructing days were becoming more frequent and were my life.

Seeing dad became virtually non-existent. He was having a great time with the girl clubs in both London and New York still, until he got completely out of NY. He started to look elsewhere in Europe so that when he pulled out of America completely, he would still have more than one club. He branched out into Paris.

This was a great venue, and one I did get to visit a couple of times, it was very classy and very French. The back wall of the bar was a wall of smoked glass mirrors with what I think were ornate perfume bottles on shelves. He eventually got out of North America completely, and the main reason was the economy, which was struggling on both sides of the Atlantic. As the London club was the backbone for all the clubs he built, the USA almost broke him.

He rallied by getting Paris going and was still looking for another venue in another European town. So his travelling days weren't just to Mallorca, which I noticed he could do at the drop of a hat, but to come visit me in Aylesbury was like going to Mars! I was learning that dad did have a selfish streak, as helpful and supportive as he was, he still treated his time outside of the club as if he was the centre of the universe and that you had to go to him...

Okay, that's not strictly true, but more often than not he just didn't want to go anywhere that he thought might be boring, and he would draw a conclusion without thinking how it might affect others. But this was what living with an ambitious and clever person was like. Like many of those who run their own business, you have to push the right buttons for them to get them excited about anything you want them to do.

My dad's generosity was huge. He frequently gave money to charity, went to charity functions, and if there was an auction, he would provide a prize but also bid on the big prizes too. He also helped me a lot. But never anything frivolous.

On my birthdays, sometimes he would forget when it was, but always got me something nice. One time, I think it was my 30th, and I was having a small party at Strings with just a few close friends. Mum wasn't there because she was in South Carolina. But dad gave me £30,000 to spend on a new car.

I was full of ideas and was hell-bent on getting a Porsche. I nearly got one that looked like dad's old Turbo and was called a 911 turbo 2. It was a left-hand drive import, and I only didn't get it because being knowledgeable and also that I had a friend in the business of Porsche car sales to come with me to have a good look. We both realised that the car was known as a ringer.... basically, a fake Porsche. It was going for just under £30,000. But I walked away and bought a Honda Integra type-R instead and saved myself £10,000 in the process.

Dad was very shocked that I didn't go the Porsche route, but impressed I'd been sensible. When he saw the car I had got, he thought it was nice but a little odd, too. Not his kind of car. But I was both happy and grateful for his help.

Something else crept up, that when the new millennium came around, I started seeing a very nice woman, and things progressed very quickly, to the point that only after 6 months of seeing each other we magically discovered we were going to be parents. This was great news to my mum, who had been despairing of not being a grandmother yet, though I was now 34 years old.

My dad took the other view at first, as his first words to the news were... "Are you going to go through with it?"

Not the most encouraging words to hear from your dad, but he was doing what he always did, thought about it from his perspective. But Sophy and I had talked a lot after she broke the news to me, and I was very happy about it. A night out to celebrate was organised, Mum and Dad, out together with Sophy and I.

We went to a restaurant, Joe Allen's in London I seem to recall it was, we had a lovely night, but when the subject of names for our baby came up, dad had a strange suggestion for if it was a boy.

"If it is a boy, I think you should call him Cisco!" Where that came from, I'll never know. I think it might have been the champagne talking and stirring up his sense of humour. Mind you, he went on to come out with another stunner... "when he is old enough, you should send him to Eaton." That was the posh school that usually turned out statesmen, and in some cases prime ministers, "And I will pay for it!" was his proclamation.

Our mouths dropped open. I started laughing... "Dad, when he is old enough, he will go where he feels happy."

He did one of his good impressions of being shocked that we were not taking him seriously, but he couldn't keep it up and cracked one of his little smiles. That was a funny night, and we ended up going to the club for a bit, before we headed home again.

Once our son Thomas was born, dad was chuffed to bits with him, and fine about his name too, as we added the middle name of 'James' which is something of a tradition within the

Stringfellow side of the family. That's because my Dad's father's name was James even though everyone called him Jim. My middle name is James too, as was my dad's.

Within a few years, Sophy and I got married, and we had the wedding in a really nice place. As neither of us were religious we had it in a Tythe Barn and had everything there. From ceremony to wedding dinner to the evening reception, it was great not having to move around too much. Dad came along with his then girlfriend, not the one who was in Ibiza. My mum came obviously and all of Sophy's side, plus a few close friends of ours and our son, which felt kind of a traditional thing as I was at my mum and dad's wedding.

The speeches were all great, but just before the evening reception/disco was to start, my dad was trying to leave. Both Sophy and I had to persuade him to stay, but I think I knew what he was trying to retreat from, which was when my mum got drunk, she would take the social monitor off and generally speak her mind and have fun. Dad obviously didn't want to be in the firing line, or his girlfriend for that matter. But a compromise was reached, he sent his girlfriend away in his limo.

He relaxed and even danced with my mum, which was brave. When it came down to it, he and my mum were still friends, even to the point that he would ring her sometimes, sometimes while drunk, mostly while sober, but mostly when he was on his own.

A year later, after our wedding, Sophy and I had a daughter, we called her Isabelle, and this time he kept quiet about names.

13

JUST A LITTLE STEP BACK

When I knew my firstborn was coming, I realised I needed to step up a gear with the work, and I embarked on trying to work every weekday at a racetrack as much as I could. I know that sounds odd to anyone who works 9 to 5, 5 days a week. But in motor racing instructing circles, it doesn't work like that.

As a self-employed instructor, you need to work for one of the main racing schools and then try work on other days when they are not operating. This is a juggling act, and your ultimate game plan is do as many of the better-paying jobs as you can. I got quite good at it, I was working at Donington and Thruxton racing schools, with the odd visit to Palmers in Bedford, and eventually, I was doing Mercedes World too, with a liberal sprinkling of track day work to just fill in the gaps. The real bugger came when you were after manufacturer work, who were generally the best payers.

Sometimes booking ahead without upsetting your bread and butter work was hard, but unlike some other guys in the same job, I didn't cancel one job because a better paying one jumped up on a day you had already committed to. I couldn't do that, mainly because it was an industry that was very close nit, and the word would get around. Sure enough the one you binned wouldn't be impressed.

My dad was very impressed with my work ethic, and he was proud of my achievement of being, though I say so myself, a very good instructor. He still tried to get me involved with the clubs more, but I was happy in my work. I could feel the stresses of the job building up, but you keep that shit to yourself.

My dad was always amazed I hadn't got into car dealing, because that's what he thought I'd be good at. I didn't agree, so I stuck at the instructing. I often wonder if had I asked dad, would he have helped me get going. I'm sure he would, but I was very happy on track, and I didn't want to sit in a garage all day waiting for someone to come in and buy a car.

I managed to get into a little safety car work just before I met Sophy, for the British Superbikes series. I had a bit of fun doing that, but it was only for a few races. A few years down the line, I got asked to do a safety car job again, this time for the British Touring Cars Championship.

Wow! That was a big gig, and of course I went for it. Dad was pleased, though a little unsure what that was about. Once I had explained it being the car in front who dictates that pace while the circuit is cleaned up where an accident had been, where the race director decided it was correct to use us because the accident was left in a dangerous enough position and that I was being paid to do it. He was happy, more so that I was getting paid rather than spending.

That was also the reason why he thought being a racing instructor was good, because I was being paid to do something I enjoyed. Don't think he ever realised that being an instructor was way more dangerous than racing myself! But that was Dad for you!

Dad and his driving

I have told you plenty about some of the wonderful cars that dad has had, and a few more are coming. But never gone into detail about his driving. I will say straight away I didn't get my talent for driving from him.

He was terrible, he was always distracted on the road; his mind was generally somewhere else. But also, he did try to do the odd daring thing. Now his generation came from when cars were a luxury and then they were mainly not very quick cars. Flash cars on the road were rare, but as he became more successful, his cars became more interesting and let's not forget that in the 70's when he really got into cars, there were no speed cameras, and not until 1965 was there a speed limit introduced. Even then it was experimental. By 1967 a maximum of 70 mph became law, but until that point, there was no limit. The first motorway was made in 1959, the M1.

Then again there weren't many cars on the road that were comfortable to go faster than 70 anyway. Yes, he did get pulled by the police for drink driving but got away with it until the afore-mentioned London incident. He sometimes showed me that his car was fast. Sometime in 1976, we were going somewhere in his Jensen Interceptor Mk3, probably to Sheffield to pick up my sister, but dad saw a police car sat on a motorway slip road, and he said, "See that police car?"

I did. He then said, "watch this!" whereupon he put his foot down and the huge V8 engine roared into life. He gave his little laugh, obviously, he'd tried this before and had lost them.

But this time... they didn't move, maybe they didn't see him, or they decided it wasn't worth trying to catch a car that they knew was way quicker than their own panda car. I think he was a little disappointed they didn't give chase... And anyway, he eased off because his challenge was not met... which may have been the cause they thought of? It has to be said he also had something else on his car that was a rare occurrence, a private plate. STR II was pretty easy to see, note and then follow up on if need be. But nobody came looking as far as I know.

Some years later when we lived in Cheshire, Dad had his first Porsche which was the 3.3-litre Turbo. Whilst I was in the front passenger seat with on the way home from somewhere and add to that a light amount of snow on the floor, we came to a T-junction that turned onto our road near home.

Again, came the words "watch this Scotty!" He then gave the throttle a stab and turned into the road, instantly the rear end slid round and he quickly shuffled the wheel round and only just caught it, as on the opposite side of the road was a post box. Had he not backed off the throttle, we would have smacked into it. Again, his laugh came out but only after a moment of slight panic when it was obvious he had tried to do something he'd only done before on his own, but without an audience and most likely was lucky to catch it then.

Whenever dad drove anywhere, his mind was usually some-where else. Not just the clubs, but if he saw premises for sale that he passed on the road, his head would swivel and, quite alarmingly, so would his arms on the steering wheel as they followed his head turn. As far as I know, he never had an accident, but he probably caused loads!

When he had someone to talk to, and he had stuff on his mind, he was way worse. Once while in Mallorca, Sophy and I were out with Dad and Bella on our way to a restaurant in Palma. We were all in his huge Mercedes ML320 which was black, had blacked out rear windows and large Brabus design wheels and chunky Pirelli off-road type tires on.

He was chatting with me about something as I was in the front with him as he drove. As I did quite naturally at the time, I was part leaning across the car just like I did when instructing, and also, I was watching the mirrors I could see. It's a habit I've never really lost when being a passenger. We came to some traffic lights which were on a three-lane bit of road, and as we moved off, I saw to our right a small Fiat 500 alongside us. It had got away from the lights at the same pace as us. Keep in mind my dad's car is high up, thanks to his ridiculously large wheels, and dad started to move across into that small car's lane. I quickly put my hand across and pushed the steering wheel back because we were on our way to crashing into them.

"Oh, Shit, Dad!" I said as I moved my hand across to keep us in our lane.

He went mad!

"Scott, you should never do that, that's very dangerous!"

"Dad, you nearly crashed into the car beside us!" was my stern, but not quite as laud reply.

"What car?"

"That small Fiat you didn't see, that's what car!" As the small Fiat just nosed ahead of us in its lane still.

He calmed down quickly, and there was a moment where he didn't know what to say, but still managed, "But still, Scotty you shouldn't do that!" The trouble with dad and I, we were not very good at backing down.

"Dad, I do a lot of car driver saving in my line of work, and I thought it better to prevent an accident if I can, rather than let it happen... don't you think? I saw it coming, you didn't!"

He grudgingly agreed, but I honestly don't remember if he apologised for my intervention or not, but he must have done, he would only say sorry if the evidence was obvious enough.

I didn't push the point, nor did I mention how stupid it was to have such a high car in Mallorca, off-road driving wasn't really in his mind. It was just dad's subtle way of making his presence felt, even on the road.

When he first started settling into Mallorca, he would hire a car, or borrow one from a friend while he was living off his boat. After all, if he wanted to go into Palma, a taxi was good enough. Later on, he would get a cheap Suzuki Vitara to leave on the pontoon as tender to his boat. But he once had a hire car in the early days he got a Mercedes A-Class. The first ones were small and had an interesting gearbox that you could have as an automatic or a sort of semi-manual. Lots of cars have this now. Mercedes still have it. Porsche has their own version too.

But on this one you could move the gear lever left and right to change up or down a gear. Dad had Sophy and I with him. I noticed, as I'd worked with these cars on Mercedes track days, he had the A-Class with this option. So, I slid my hand down to the lever, which was situated slightly further back than a normal gear lever would be. As he drove, we chatted, and I started changing gear at the right points for him. He was blissfully unaware I was doing this. I started to comment how this car was quite good for a small car and was quite responsive.

He agreed that it seemed pretty nippy, and he was wondering what to buy, and did I think he should get one? Though he wasn't so sure about the styling. I mentioned again how it was really quite good, "especially when you move the gear lever around like this"

He took a quick look down as I flicked the lever again to show him. "Scotty what are you doing, don't you're gonna break it," was his stern surprised cry.

I laughed! "Dad, I've been working with these a few times this year on Mercedes track days, they are supposed to be used like this if you want to use it as a manual."

The look on dad's face at first was shock, but quickly subsided into a moment of being unsure, then a small grin followed by "Scotty, you little rotter!" then quickly followed by curiosity and of course he wanted a go.

After not changing when you should... we put it back to auto mode, as he really wasn't sure about it.

As for when he drove anywhere in London, he was king of fiddling with the various controls in the car, especially when he got another Porsche. The Carrera S4 convertible was a lovely car, and I really loved it. Lucky for me I got to drive it a lot too, but he also got the benefit of that by me being the one who filled it with fuel more than him. My tours were out of London more often than he.

Dad did shorter journeys, mainly from his apartment on the south bank of the River Thames, for the five-minute drive to the club. He really didn't watch the road well, and on occasion, he would not stop for a red light, which drove me mad. Also, he would fiddle with the sat-nav or phone controls.

Sometimes he would stop in the middle of the street when traffic was moving slowly to look at a shop or other premises that had a "for sale" board outside, which infuriated me. He was oblivious to anyone else, just start to have a conversation about what could be done on that plot. He'd think nothing about coming to a complete stop when fiddling with the air climate controls which would get the car behind hitting its horn.

One time he was about to get in his Porsche parked outside our Soho club, he turned to me and asked in all seriousness... "Do you think this is too much for me, do you think I do it justice?"

I was amazed, as dad was so confident about everything he did.

"Dad, you're Peter Stringfellow, the undisputed King of Clubs... people expect you to have a nice car, don't worry about it. But if you want to change it, just do it. You don't have to prove anything!"

He really thought about getting a Bentley convertible, which would have been perfect for him, but there was one problem. He lived in an apartment block, and the underground garage area was accessed via a small car lift system. His Porsche just about fit in fine, but a Bentley would have been a different story, so I told him.

"Dad, you need to move to a new house with your own garage first for a Bentley, the first time you try getting a Bentley in the lift, you may just bump it on the way in... and then you'll hate it!" I reasoned.

He agreed, but was very keen on changing, which he did in the end. I think it was the act of being in his 70's and getting in and out of a low sports car that was getting to him. So, he swapped to a Range Rover Evoque, which was much easier to get in and out of, and he was happy again. I missed the Porsche, but it was dad's car, I couldn't afford a Porsche that's for sure.

14

SWAP INSTRUCTING LIFE FOR NIGHTLIFE AND DAD MOVES OUT OF TOWN

I was getting through life ok, but the instructing was becoming quite hard for some reason, I really was finding it hard to keep on top of the self-employed lifestyle of forever chasing work to keep the money coming in. I had a wife, who worked too, two kids a mortgage and a lot of road mileage covered, not to mention the god knows how many miles covered on racetracks.

It was the constant repetition I think, that got to me. A few years back I had tried to break away from it, and I had a stint of being trained up to be a DJ at Strings, but the resident DJ back then must have thought I was after his job, as he didn't teach me much. So, I went back to instructing, but that was when I was alone and had no bills to face.

Things were different now. At Thruxton, I was in a lovely Ferrari 355 every day and taught about 20 to 23 people a day at four laps each of the right way to get around the circuit in this effortlessly quick car. And until I stopped at Donington I was part of the team of instructors that taught groups of people, mostly corporate groups and then some that were wanting to complete the racing school course. Again, with many laps in the cars as I sat next to 3-4 people in the car across an hour for each small group, roughly 15 minutes each before they moved onto the next activity elsewhere at the track.

Track days were different, but in some way the same depending on which track day company you were working for. My favourite was RMA. I met good people and managed to pace myself throughout the day with the added bonus of driving or being driven in some of the most amazing cars shit loads of money could buy, and I wasn't paying for the fuel for them either. There were a few other track day groups I worked for, but RMA took me to some great tracks in Europe too.

Then there were the manufacturer days, which were the most sort after. They paid very well, and were well structured, though they were not meant to be about going as fast as possible. They were meant to show the manufacturers fleet of cars off in a controlled and safe environment. Though that didn't stop some people with an instructor pushing them on, to go pretty quickly. Though no instructor let a customer go quicker than they could handle, but sometimes you would get someone in who didn't want to listen to instruction and usually screwed up enough to spin or at worst crash the car.

Those days were generally great as you got to drive a lot of very nice new cars, and I drove for most manufacturers of every kind of car in my time of instructing. I even got Dad and Bella along to a Jaguar day at the Millbrook test facility, as dad was thinking of getting a Jag again. I looked after dad, and he had to let Bella be looked after by one of my fellow instructing colleges, which I think my dad was a little reticent about. But he soon relaxed and enjoyed the day.

Generally, I was forever on the road going to a track somewhere, up early, drive over an hour or so to the circuit, sit with people all day concentrating and never shutting up as I gave my info into the intricacies of driving on a racetrack. Then drive home again half knackered, before doing it all again the next day.

I could feel the tediousness of it all growing inside me. I was getting agitated. My only freedom was being at home in the evenings and doing Safety Car with BTCC. I have to add I also started doing safety Car for a new racing series called A1GP. That was brilliant too, as I travelled the world on that gig. I was back to living a life of never seeing dad.

On one of the away races with A1GP I was in New Zealand and with a week's gap before we moved on to Australia, and I got to do a bit of sightseeing. I found myself on a chair lift heading up to the base station of a visitor centre halfway up a volcano when I got the idea to call dad up on my mobile phone. It was a great moment, as he was just on his way into the club when I rang him and told him "Hey dad, I'm halfway up a volcano on a chair lift, it's called Mount Ruapehu, and it last erupted in 1996. How cool is this?"

He got straight away how this must have felt, and he was equally blown away that I had called him not just from halfway up a sleeping volcano but also from the other side of the world. It's one of those memories that has stuck in my mind forever, to hear his voice from so far away.

I think dad got a kick out of the fact that I was travelling so much and seeing more of the world. And when the race series finished after its first year, we did a deal with A1GP to have the party after the awards night in London to be held at my dad's Soho club "Peter Stringfellows Angels."

It had gone through a few renames before he settled on that name for it. We did a deal that saw the logo "STRINGFEL-LOWS" on the rear engine cover on the Team GB car for the final meeting at Brands Hatch where it managed a win for the last race of the year.

The Stringfellows logo has only ever been on three race cars, and two of the races it was in were wins, this one and on my car at Donington in 1989. Dad came to the doo, and it was all great fun too.

Unfortunately, A1GP folded after nearly three years, and I had stopped after two years as the races started clashing with BTCC, and I wasn't about to stop with touring cars, as it had been going for nearly 60 years at that point.

I was getting ever wearier with the instructing, which I surprised myself with, as one of my instructing friends had observed once that I was a "lifer". He was nearly right, because I was up to 21 years of being an instructor. Which goes to show that you never can plan ahead too much because your own feelings can change.

I asked dad if he would want me to get involved more with the clubs, which was fine by him. So for a short time, I was instructing and working at night, and just to add more to my life I got into doing my own radio show for Radio Silverstone, which I called "Formula String".

Radio Silverstone was going to be 24 hours a day station playing music and motor racing-based shows. I got into it and had a great time. Dad was quite impressed with that. But worried as I was looking after the kids on the Wednesday, diving off to do my show LIVE for two hours once my wife was back from work, then I was off to work. Crazy way to live.

I changed my night off to that night to suit it. But after a couple of years of that madness, I stepped out of it. Meanwhile back in 2009, I made plans to stop instructing and commit to the club life for real. Mind you 2009 wasn't just a big step for me. Dad was going to get married again!

We knew dad would end up getting married to Bella. We could tell it was different with her. Sure enough, he let us all know they planned on getting married on the 14th of February. He freely admitted that the reason for holding it on Valentine's Day was to ensure he wouldn't forget the date. But also they were going to do the ceremony in Barbados, which was a surprise.

However they were going to be inviting family and select friends to join them there, too. This was great news, and dad asked me to be best man. The icing on the cake was that Sophy, the kids and I were going to make it into a family holiday too by staying on for two weeks, which was brilliant. The Wedding was held at the Almond Beach Resort, with all family and friends present. There was an old, slightly derelict sugar mill within the grounds that had been cleaned up and used for weddings. The setting was beautiful, and it was a lovely day. Dad and I wore white suits, my daughter, who was five years old at the time was the flower girl, who walked ahead of the bride spreading flower petals on the ground up to the altar. She was very cute.

I did my job and handed over the rings when asked. I saw dad get a little emotional, which was a surprise. And once the man and wife bit was done, we all went off to the beach for drinks and photos, which was fantastic. And dad being dad, he got HELLO magazine to cover it, and we were in a lovely photo that was taken and used in the magazine.

Dad and Bella were staying at a private villa called the "The Green Monkey Villa." As the name suggests there were monkeys in the area who would visit the back garden. The place was more like a palace than a hotel. Dad had really sorted out all his contacts for this. The whole trip was amazing, and once they had all left the island, we had a lovely family holiday that even to this day the kids remember fondly.

Later in the year I made plans to drop the instructing life, and I decided that my last instructing work was going to be special. I got asked by Prodrive, a car performance company who I had been working for on and off for the last few years and who even had their own track to help run a track day. It would be for Aston Martin owners at the Belgian racetrack

Spa-Francorchamps, which if you remember, is my most favourite track of all the tracks I had been on. So that was going to be a fitting way to bow out. The two-day event came and went in a flash and was one I would love to have included my dad on. And then I got involved with the clubs for real.

The transition to nightlife was going to be a hard one, but dad made it easy for me. He let me arrive late, usually around 10:30 at night, and I would leave sometime around 3 a.m. When I joined the operating hours were 9 p.m. to 3:30 a.m. Years before when we were a disco, we would close by 3 a.m.

To change your hours around from day light living was pretty hard on me, and also hard on my wife. I would be working full nights with one night off a week. After I gave up the Radio Show, I changed my night off to the Saturday so I could spend time with my kids more, as the hours were eating into my home life. It was a huge change alright and adjustments took time.

My Dad made a big change of his own. He decided as he now had a baby daughter with Bella, he needed to be out of town and not living in an apartment. This was a great idea; I and others had been telling him he needed to be further out of London to have a proper home life if he was having young children to.

It had been so long since he was living far from the club, not counting his trips to Mallorca that is, because by now he had a lovely house over there too. Which reminds me of a time when my family and I went out to be with him in Mallorca for a holiday and while at the villa one night, after having dinner on the patio that overlooked a stunning view of the town below and the port. He and I went for a swim in the pool he had. We were talking, and I commented on how wonderful the house was, and that it must feel great to own it.

He looked round at one point and to look up at the house from the water and he said "I worked hard for this kind of lifestyle, and yeah.... I think I earned it!" He didn't say it in any belligerent way, just a relaxed realisation and appreciation of his 50 years of working his way up to this life he had.

His house move in England took him to just outside the M25 in Gerrard's Cross. It was a large house, with its own driveway and double garage. He was ready to remember what it was like to live outside a busy city again. This was a lovely house too. It was funny to think how against the idea he was at first. I really do think he was joined at the hip to the clubs a little too much. But once he was settled outside of London, he got it... and even started to look like he wanted to retire sooner rather than later.

That was a monumental change for him. Another change was that I, on occasion, would swing by his house on my way into work and pick him up, sometimes in my car, sometimes we went in his. It was a golden opportunity to talk about many things, which we did. Sometimes about my goings-on, and sometimes things going off in the world in general, never about racing unless he instigated it, which was usually something he saw on the news formula one related perhaps.

And we talked about the clubs, ideas, customers we knew and a lot about those that worked in the clubs too. It was on these journeys of just being him and I that I really got to know a whole other new side of dad. I had always known he was forthright, and he was the one who had the final word on everything in the club. But dad asked my opinion or view on some of the staff within the club, and as I had been thrust into the security side by learning all about the CCTV system we had, which was mandatory for our licence to operate, it was written in stone by the council.

Dad learned that I was very observant, but I did make the odd mistake too in my early days, as I was used to acting straight away to an incident because of the very nature of my instructing life. Holding back or hesitation could land you in hospital at best or killed at worst.

But dad drilled into me the value of learning to sit back, see how things unfolded, let a more senior manager deal with it and watch. And if I got wind of a problem, I was to be close by, again to watch and see how things were done.

His advice and insights were priceless, and he also could read when social attitudes were changing. Add to that his understanding of the business as a whole. He was amongst the first to see how the social picture was changing for attitudes to our kind of business and that our social pitch was aimed at the corporate high-flyer.

Mind you the stigma that had been made over many years dating back as far as the 40s and 50s about our kind of club, which had been dubbed a "strip club" long before dad brought the classier version from a more accepting America did have its effect. There were many in social circles ready to stamp on dad as he changed from disco King of Clubs to the impresario of jumping into a new direction. But these people had never set foot in his clubs, so didn't see the difference. They also were ready to brand him as a "dirty old man" which couldn't be further from the truth. Granted he had developed a taste for younger women, but with wealth and a glittering personality like his, he did attract them. He rarely chased someone, they generally fell for him, and as they were all beautiful women, he went with it.

But his advice for me when I got back in with the clubs, I say got back in, but the truth was, I'd never fully left. His advice was "Don't play around with the girls Scotty, they need to respect you and your position, and you need to respect them. Their job isn't easy."

And he was right, however he forgot something. I didn't want a girl that was too young, and at this point, I was still married and at home. Sure, I met one or two that got my pulse racing, and yes, my male genes were shouting at me, but dad was right, and I saw its effects first hand as someone else within the business, quite high up too, was taking huge advantage of some of the girls. Ultimately, he lost his job because of it.

I learned to get over the initial pangs of a rampant male, and quickly developed a shell against letting my testosterone get the better of me. At the end of the day, they were at work, and they needed to feel confident that I wasn't there to make the job harder for them. I felt that leading by example was also going to rub off on the others. Because when your family name is over the door, you are a target, you are watched, you are the one they look at waiting for you to make the mistakes to make it alright for others. I decided not to make those mistakes.

Dad and I talked a lot on those drives into work, about every-thing and everyone in the club. Sometimes I asked difficult questions, but to his credit, he answered them. He never shied away from much.

I learnt a lot. The golden one was "keep your eyes and ears open and your mouth shut... But tell me later, learn all you can and remember there will be a lot of nothing happening, but when it all gets going, be ready." It took me awhile to realise what he meant by that, but I got there in the end.

When dad walked into the club, his GM would be waiting, and he would walk with him. All the time Dad's eyes were taking everything in. He missed nothing: The lighting level, the sound level, where things were placed, where the girls were sat, who wasn't paying attention and who was.

Walking into the club was like breathing to him, it was second nature to feel everything was right, and if it wasn't right... he pointed it out. He never fraternised with the girls, and they knew not to go up to him. He was the Boss, but he was approachable, and he was congenial with customers, whom it has to be said, all treated him with huge respect. When we had two clubs, he always went to both, unless he had dinner at Stringfellows that went on too long. His days of being boisterous and full of energy until the early hours were long gone, he was usually away back home by about 1 a.m., sometimes earlier.

On the subject of time, dad made another adjustment. We began to close at 3:30 a.m. for a while. Which was fine, and then about a year on from that we stayed open until 4:30 a.m. This was tough on staff, but the spenders were staying later. One of our GM's decided he couldn't cope with that and left the company due to "stress." But we all knew he just couldn't do the extra hour. Something else started to happen too. My dad's brother Geoff had been diagnosed with Alzheimer's disease, which was a huge blow to my dad. But then Geoff had been a problem for dad for many years as he had been a chronic alcoholic, to the point that he took drastic measures to stay off the drink. But this was something else, Geoff was to be on the road to a steady decline.

Dad looked after everybody in his family, he took massive gambles in his life, but he still looked after his family.

We stayed at 4:30 for a while, but not too long later another director within the company floated the idea of staying open until 5:30. I knew this was going to be a problem, but the other dickhead of a director convinced dad that spenders were still out there until the stupid hours of the morning. I saw the effect this had on staff, effectively this was taking away an hour of the staff's normal life, and some had kids.

I felt it too as my drive to work was an hour and that drive back was harder, as by the time I got out which was closer to 6 a.m., I wasn't getting home until after 7. I let Dad know about this and how it was affecting not just me, but everyone. He always left by about 1 so didn't see how things were at 5, let alone 5:30. The underground trains didn't restart until 5:30, so we had people sat in the club, not spending but nursing drinks until the club closed. It was soul-destroying.

After a few months of this I embarked on getting dad to see sense, which eventually he agreed, and we all went back to 4:30. I still thought that was a rubbish time, but the customers were still happy, so we kept at that, though personally I would have been happier to stop at 4 . The other senior director wasn't happy, but then again, he wasn't in the club until the end of the night either.

There was something I noticed about dad at this time. He seemed in a bad mood a lot of the time. And when we had our management meetings at the Soho club, he was always in a difficult mood. We would be waiting for Dad and the other senior directors to come into the room, more often than not the other managers and I would be either talking to each other or fiddling with our mobiles. I used to bring my Autosport magazine, which when Dad arrived, I would put down on the table, to which point he would see it and make a comment, usually a cutting one.

That used to confuse me, as it was doing no harm. It wasn't until much later at the hospital that I worked out why he was that way.

Our management meetings were always very open, and if you had a gripe, now was the time to air it. He listened to opinions, and didn't mind the odd heated discussion because as far as he was concerned it was better out than in.

Dad was a great person to work for. He would also have "dancers' meetings" which was held at the Covent Garden club, with all the girls summoned surrounding the stage while dad was on stage reading his notes out, sometimes just to pep the girls up and reminding them that the club cared about them too.

These meetings went a long way to creating unity within the club's main asset, the girls. Some of the meetings were very funny, with Dad doing impressions of things that some of the girls shouldn't do or say. His impression of a bored dancer on a pole looking at her watch was a really good one and impressed upon them the importance of the poles as a show more than just something you had to do.

He was brilliant at keeping them part of the whole team. Many girls would be with us for years, because they felt safe and part of the fabric of the club. He also had a favourite saying about the customers... He would tell the girls to treat the customers, no matter how old or not as attractive, treat them all as if they are Brad Pitt!

Brothers

Dad, as I have said, looked after everyone. And as the eldest brother, he watched over them too. When things for them got bad, he was there for all of them. Geoff's Alzheimer's was getting worse, to the point where he had to go to a hospice to be looked after 24/7. It was too much for his own wife.

Paul was next in line below Geoff in age and had been part of the clubs for literally years, he had been my dad's bars manager for the last four night clubs and had even done a stint at Geoff's own club up in Manchester that dad helped Geoff set up after they stopped being partners.

One night in the office at Stringfellows I was talking with my Uncle Paul, and he said something that I can't quite remember now, but my reply was, "Ah, but you're not keen though are you" to which his reply was "How do you know about that?"

"About what?' I said with a scowl... we were the only two in the office, and I realised instantly this was something important I'd stumbled onto.

Paul wasn't quick enough to cover it up, and in all honesty, I think he was relieved to get it out.

"About the chemo I've got to have," was his reply.

I was stunned "Err... you have Cancer?... does dad know about this?"

Paul looked uncomfortable "Well, no... he's got enough on. He doesn't need my problems on his plate as well does he."

"Paul, he's your brother, and he cares and if he can help, you know he will. Besides he needs to know and if you don't tell him, I will. But he would prefer it to come from you."

Paul sighed and knew I was right. Later that night I saw Paul take dad to the back of the staircase on the ground floor, I could see from a distance he was telling dad. I felt both sad, but glad he had told him. The next day dad did exactly what I knew he would do, he got Paul to see dad's very expensive but very efficient and fast private doctor Dr. Barry Grimaldi. The NHS is brilliant, but sometimes speed isn't their strong point, mainly because they have so many patients to care for. Private healthcare is expensive, but a lot quicker for test results.

His other brother Terry wasn't having a good time of it either, he had been an alcoholic quietly for some time and had got involved with the wrong kind of people on and off. Terry had been a problem for quite some time. It's no exaggeration, unfortunately, to say Terry was ignorant, greedy, huge ego and thick. I never really got on with Terry, I knew too much about him and the way he treated his own dad, and how much of a small-time crook he was to his own brothers.

But dad did his best to help him, guide him and pretty much protect him as only he knew how. Terry could take and abuse every kind deed. Eventually, he was stuck in a hospital with a chronic weight condition, and liver trouble thanks to all the drink. Dad took all this in his stride.

Geoff and Paul were his immediate priority. Dad himself had had a brush with cancer some years before and had it treated so quickly and so well, he was cleared within a short time, but it had cost him half a lung. Which was surprising as he never smoked, but before the laws were changed about smoking indoors, dad had spent many years breathing in other people's smoke, I guess. However, his fast recovery was mainly down to his great health cover and speed of treatment. He extended that privilege to the rest of his family as much as he could.

15

THE CALM BEFORE THE STORM

Working with dad was interesting, as he never made it look like work. He had a certain way with everything. He honed this talent from very early on I guess, as dad grew in his knowledge and gift of getting to know people who later on, we would come to know as legends in their art, field, genre, or call it what you want. These people he got to know on their collective way up, which in turn introduced him to other famous people. When that happened, he was considered an equal.

But sometimes he could act strange when I was with him as he mixed with other celebrities he knew. There was a bachelor party that was going to be thrown at dad's Soho club Angels. It was for Russell Brand, the well-known stand-up comedian. His guest list was a who's who of comedy and a famous musician. Jonathan Ross, Rob Brydon, Jimmy Carr, David Baddiel and Steve Coogan were there with Noel Gallagher as part of the crew too.

They all behaved themselves it has to be said, as they were all very aware that how they acted in public could be shared round the world in seconds as everyone had a phone on them that could record and be sent wherever. I was hoping to be introduced to most if not all of them, but as I hung near dad, he seemed to act very strangely and acted as if I wasn't there. He didn't introduce me to anyone.

It got to the point where they would flick their eyes at me as if to say... "er, mate who the fuck are you?... I'm talking to Peter here." I got quite embarrassed at one point and just walked away. But later I just introduced myself and had a nice chat with Jonathan and David. I got a little too relaxed when I saw Jimmy Carr and called him Alan instead... as at the time there was another funny man who was quite camp called Alan Carr. But Jimmy didn't say anything, but for some reason took on an American accent.

It was only after he went away did, I suddenly realise I had called him Alan instead of Jimmy! That did it for me, and I quietly moved away from the group acutely embarrassed now. At least I recovered enough to stand with dad and Noel for a bit, and at least got to say hello. But I was starting to feel like a hovering mad fan, and so I took a walk over to the other club. I never mentioned it to dad, and I now wish I had.

There were occasions that unfolded into great experiences. One such time was when the well-known stage and TV actor Robert Lindsey walked into the club. He was literally walking by when he saw the club and as he said, "I've not been in there since the 80s and thought... well, why not... I wonder if Peter is in?"

He asked if dad was in at reception and as they recognised him, he walked through and was led up to dad's table, where dad was both surprised and pleased to see him. They both sat and chatted for a long time. He had been to an awards doo and was passing by. Dad introduced me to him, and we talked at length about many things. I told him I'd been to see his sitcom "My Family" being filmed at the studio in Elstree.

He was a great laugh, and though not getting involved with any of the girls, not even for one dance. He was looking at his watch and started to fret about missing his train back home. Dad offered for us to take him home later if he wanted to stay longer. It was on the way to my dad's house apparently.

He agreed and just sat with dad and had a great time, eventually the time came to go. As we got to the car, I noticed Robert was quite sloshed, as is normal when you hit the outside air, the body reacts. He got in the back and I drove with dad in the front too. As we pulled away, Robert asked the question that I've heard people ask him a million times. "Peter, how did you get into this business?"

Dad knew there was two versions to this question... how did he start in the beginning, or how did he get into the "girl club" life?

Robert was asking about how he got into the Gentleman's club side, which dad launched into. I'd heard this in his company a few times, but it was always good to listen again, because he always added something else that wasn't in the story the last time. So, I drove, and he talked, and Robert listened. Eventually dad stopped and then asked, "Does that answer your question? Robert.... Robert?"

I leaned up a little to look in the rear-view mirror, so I could see. And there was Robert... fast asleep!

"Dad, he's asleep!" I said with a sideways glance. Dad gave a small laugh "Well, I didn't think I was that boring!"

It suddenly dawned on me that I didn't have his address in the sat-nav yet. I mentioned it to dad, and he said, "Ah, he's somewhere on the way after coming off the A40, shall we ask him then?"

I thought that was a good idea, so we carried on and I asked more about his newer version of the story, because I had been listening. Eventually, we turned off the A40 and we had to wake him for the post code.

"Robert, Robert... you need to wake up!"

Robert was clearly irritated and came out of his snooze a bit short-tempered. "What...what... what?" he said clearly not with it yet.

"We need your postcode, so we can take you home..." said dad.

He rattled off the postcode, I entered it, and we got on our way... Robert went back to sleep. I followed the route, but as we got closer, I got the feeling this isn't where a successful stage and TV actor lived! It was small tight streets with vans and quite honestly, average cars, and we pulled up outside a block of flats...

We tried to wake Robert again... "Robert, is this where you live?" again he was agitated and hadn't really come around enough. "What...what? Oh yes..." he paused, took a better look and said, "Where the fuck are we?"

Dad looked at me... I said, "Robert, what's your postcode again?"

Robert was quite confused... He told me the code again and this time the numbers in the address were switched around. We were not far off, but we were in the wrong place. "Dad, he had the numbers the wrong way around before. It's ok, it's not far."

I get the car going again, and within about five minutes we were driving up a more secluded area, and eventually stopped outside some large gates with an entry phone system. This was more like it. He thanked us and sauntered a slight stagger to the gates, he put his code in and the gates opened. He waved as he walked in, and just as the gates closed dad and I broke out into laughter...

We laughed nearly all the way back to his house. It will live in my mind forever as one of those gloriously shared funny moments in my life with dad. And should I see Robert on TV acting again, I know I shall think of the night we took him home!

2017 started out well, but became eventful in many ways, both good and bad.

In the back end of January Dad and I went out to Mallorca, a break without family, just he and I. He was thinking of selling his magnificent villa as he had bought a place in the south of Italy. He was thinking of moving all his stuff to the Italian place, or to sell furniture in Palma, or even take what he needed and then sell the place part furnished.

For some reason, I decided to take photos of the house inside and out. I got quite a collection, and I loved the place anyway. We also did all the usual things of visiting cafés and restaurants. With a smattering of cooking at home. It was great and a nice wind down from the hours I worked.

Dad, for the most part, was agonising over the change. I really think he was thinking ahead and was trying to give Bella and my younger brother and sister a place to go near Bella's mother who was Italian and lived out there.

We had a good time out there, and it was further bonding dad and I, but the club had sort of done that. I wasn't just the chauffer. On the journey back, we had the usual problem of dad's personal impatience for queuing and he was a nightmare to be with. Which explains in part why he was usually late for a plane. He would become very strange and impatient. He hated queuing for anything.

Once back in Jolly England it was back to work and planning ahead for BTCC work for me. And dad got on with heading up the club as well as organising his house plans. But later in the year, a few things happened. Dad had a little run-in with cancer again, this time an infection from a problem in his bile duct.

This was quickly rectified with a procedure, a quick course of tablets and he was given the all-clear not too long after, but the visits to hospital were a scare, an all of it happened around the time of the horrendous Grenfell Tower tragedy. In fact, my sister was heading away in a limousine back to where she was staying outside the M25 and saw the flames as the traffic slowed to look at the tragic event unfold. The A40 Westway road passed by quite close to the incident. As dad was in the hospital on medication after the op, he found he couldn't watch it on the news channel in his room. He said it made him feel sick. I think it's safe to say we were all of the same feeling.

Dad got out of hospital and made a great recovery. We were all very relieved. But the ups and down of the year were not done yet. After something like ten years of decline, Geoff Stringfellow passed away in his room at the hospice. He had been bad for a while, but one day he just slipped away. This had a huge impact on Dad. It was a major blow. The funeral was so emotional, Dad got up to say a few words and just made it through but broke down at the end. It was heart breaking to see, and the second time I had seen it. He tried to say a few words at his Dad's funeral... That was harder for him.

Ironically, literally the next day, Dad and I went off to Mallorca again. This time to make some finishing touches to the Villa. It felt different being there this time, and I did a couple of Facebook live links for fun. I did a show around of the villa, and some personal silly ones, like getting in the freezing swimming pool. It was to be drained and patches of tiles fixed in it.

Dad helped me out being cameraman for one of them... it was very funny. He took the piss a lot. Then one evening when he was getting a bunch of guys over who were his Mallorca friends, or "Portals posse" as I called them, I do a thing on

Facebook live called "Cooking with String." I asked dad if he wanted to do one with me in his kitchen... He agreed, and we had a fantastic, funny time. To this day it's the most watched of my Cooking Links and I have watched some of it from time to time. In total it was two hours long, even I haven't re-watched it all... but someday I will. (After I wrote this, I watched it... loved it)

Dad also had a wall down the side of the house fixed. Honestly, this place was going to be mint by the time dad finished putting the small but tricky to fix things right.

The next day after the Cooking night, we had another problem. The kitchen sprung a leak under the sink. Very hot water was pouring out. This wasn't the first-time dad had sink trouble. But this time instead of his sink crashing through his cupboards while filming a TV cooking show (Ironically), this time it was just us. two of the most non-DIY guys you've ever seen. We managed to turn off the water at the mains tap for the hot water, which was under the sink annoyingly. We set about mopping up and cleaning up while we waited for my Dad's English handyman to arrive. We were a right pair, bare feet, shorts on and laboriously mopping and emptying buckets.

It had flooded the kitchen pretty well before it was discovered, as I only found out after going down to make a coffee. The sound of the water was pretty consistent with thinking my dad was in the shower, I'd heard it earlier and was going to ask him If he wanted a coffee, but decided to wait until after his shower... he was in there a long time, and so eventually decided to make one myself.

That's when I found the open plan kitchen swimming in water and had just started to cascade off the step down into the dining area. That was a long morning. Much later on, we went in his jacuzzi, that had taken hours to warm up, and now I think about it, that was the last time he went in it.

The next day I did more filming for my Facebook LIVE, I had a brave dip in his freezing pool, with dad as cameraman... It was pretty funny, he was taking the piss so much, but this was how our double act worked. Again, it's another memory captured on film that I will treasure forever.

On this occasion, I came back alone from Mallorca, as dad was really finalising all the official details for the house and had to stay on a bit longer. I really felt very sad about this being the last time I will have been in the house. But when I got back, I had another special trip planned. I was going to go to Florida with my kids Thomas and Isabelle. We were going to do the Universal Studios theme park in Orlando.

I had booked a resort hotel right on the doorstep, well, a small boat ride to the entrance. We were heading for the Harry Potter experience area, which was fantastic. My sister Karen was going to meet up with us on one of the days with her daughter.

Karen and I got a big kick out of wandering along with our kids ahead of us. When we were kids ourselves, we did all the American theme parks with mum and dad too. It would have been nice to do it with dad and my younger brother and sister too, but dad had done the Disney park with his wife and the little ones about a year before. Karen met up with him for that too as she lived only a couple of hours away.

When we got back after a fantastic week away, it was back to work and back to normal. Dad was still coming into the club but having to be really careful as his operation was a success but with a slower recovery. However, he organised a small birthday party at one of his favourite restaurants, the much-celebrated Langan's Brasserie in Mayfair, just close friends and family. It was a great doo. And he seemed really relaxed and happy. It was his 77th birthday.

Then about a couple of weeks later he had another op to clear things up again, and this time he got a little careless.

He literally had the small procedure in the morning, discharged from the hospital by the afternoon. And planned to go to the club in the evening. I, like everyone else, though he was bonkers. But what he wasn't telling anyone else was he planned to go look at another club for a possible takeover, to rebrand as another Stringfellows. This news was broken to us around the dinner table at Strings.

I went mad. "Dad, you've just had another operation. You shouldn't even be here, let alone go look at another premises. But he was adamant, probably because he wanted the world to know he was okay, and the potential club was on Park Lane and part of the London Hilton Hotel. I said I would drive him there and be with him.

His friend Albert was going to come with us. I wasn't happy about any of this, Dad wasn't strong enough for this kind of outing after an operation. But he could be a stubborn bugger.

We drew up outside the hotel, where I was told I could leave the car, because I said he wasn't going to be able to walk far and not going to stay too long. We had agreed that I would take him straight home after the viewing. We got out of the car and walked to the club entrance, which was next to the hotel entrance. It was a steep flight of stairs. I looked at him and said, "You have got to be fucking joking".

"Scotty, I just want to have a look, and then we will go," was his quiet but serious reply. I moved in front, so he could do his usual hand on my shoulder to climb the stairs, usually it was for going down, but I wasn't taking any chances.

As we got to the top, I felt his grip slightly tighten, then as we got to the top and saw the manager waiting for him, he quickly dropped his hand. The pretence was on. He knew people would be watching and he wanted to show a strong side, no hint of weakness. This was how he could be. He used to play poker and he was good at that. His confidence was his shield. We walked round a little... after a while, he said, "So what do you think Scotty?"

"Nice bar, but a little too small for us. Also, rather too easy for customers to invite girls up to their rooms don't you think?" I reminded him.

"Yes, you might be right. Okay, let's go." He spoke to the manger and was very polite and complimentary. We headed off back to the stairs.

Again, I took up my position and he nearly wasn't going to take it, but I reminded him, "These stairs are steep dad, there is no way you are going down without me"

He saw the logic and good job too. Just as we got to the bottom, his hand started to shake on my shoulder. But we made it out, got him into the car. As we drove off, I was pulling out into Park lane, while he got his mobile out to text Bella that he was on his way home.

As we got onto the A40 dad was in reflective mood.

"Thanks for driving me Scotty. You know, I miss driving."

Dad didn't see, but I had a lump in my throat when he said it.

"Well, when you're all better again, you can drive again."

We had talked about cars sometimes, but only if it was about cars he knew about... or if I knew something about a car he liked. We talked cars a bit, on how he would like one of those Jaguar F-Pace cars, though here I was driving him in his Jaguar XF-R Sport. Once a few years ago we both fancied having a Jaguar F-Type each. Though my personal favourites were Porsche 911s or the Panamera. He had so many great cars over the years.

I woke him once we got to his house, gave him a hug, and he went in while I got back in my car that was waiting to go back to my house.

It was while driving home that night I got to worrying about him more. After all, he'd sold his Villa and now trying to prove something by trying to go out straight after an operation. I got a niggling feeling that he was worrying a lot too, just trying not to show it.

After that night, dad seemed to do the right thing more, and didn't go into London again. He got that he needed to be much stronger for those jaunts and he wasn't there yet. One day I was overseeing him when as I was leaving, he followed me to the door, but as he got to the hallway, he leaned heavily against the bottom of the stairs against the bannister. He was okay, just a bit tired. That was a warning sign and a half to me.

He had more trips in and out of hospital. But he was on some tablets and since he chilled out seemed to be doing well. Christmas was okay. He even got to spend it with Bella and the kids. He still had one hand on the wheel with the club as everyone kept him up to speed. And then just after Christmas... all hell broke loose.

16

AFTER 'THE END' LIFE GOES ON.

7th June 2018

And here we are again... Back to the end.

From my park bench in Regents Park, I was in shock. It was a beautiful day; lot of people were just going about their lives oblivious that someone great had just died. If I'd asked any one of them, "Do you know who Peter Stringfellow is?" the odds on them knowing were high. I sat looking at the trees, plants, squirrels and people. I could hear the sounds of London just going on as it does, day in day out. I was at a loss of what to do. I was on my own, not more than 1,000 yards away from the hospital where he passed away, and only 500 yards away from where we used to live in the 80s. It was surreal on a very personal level. I don't know how long I sat there. Time didn't mean anything anymore. But at some point, I was back in my car. I needed to drive to occupy my mind. My eyes were still holding back the tears that I wanted to cry, but my stupid inner self was stopping me. Just... Drive!

I felt quite distant, I drove as if on autopilot. I felt everything happening, but I wasn't doing the thinking, another part of me was taking care of that. The racing driver and instructor side of my mind took the wheel but didn't speed. I'd had this feeling before back in 1988 when I was driving to Italy in a van to pick up steering wheels for a friend's company. He was having a sleep in the back and I was very tired. Something came over me then and literally took the wheel while I felt like I was stretching my arms out, but I could see my arms weren't moving off the wheel... It was like that only I wasn't stretching, just letting someone else drive me home.

I didn't for a second think it was my dad helping me, he wasn't great at driving, remember, so I think we can rule that one out. The next few days were crazy. I had a touring car race meeting that coming weekend at Oulton Park. I'm sure nobody would have minded if I hadn't gone, I'm sure my safety car job was safe. But I needed the racetrack to escape to, my safe, happy place. Many years ago, I taught myself to be focused at a track regardless of what was happening in my life. I needed that now.

So that weekend, I went to Silverstone to pick the Panamera up on the Friday and there was some corporate doo going on the same day at the Porsche Experience Centre where I used to pick the car up from, there was a photographer with an old 911 doing instant photos for guests, or whatever reason, I had a picture taken. And as I think about it now, I know I looked a bit distant in it. I picked up the Panamera and took it home, from there I went up to the track the next day.

Saturday morning, I arrived at Oulton Park with Pete Harris, my wingman and Safety Car observer, was being great and understood where I was. In the paddock, many people came up to me to offer their condolences. And strange as it seems I felt like I had a shell on, I felt like I was floating through the day. Some people obviously were very surprised to see me, and others completely got why I was there.

I managed to get through the first day without any problems, and even on the Sunday, which was race day, I did really well. A very old school friend whom I'd not seen for over 40 years came to the race with her son. It was lovely to see

Sarah Roberts, who I had been at school within the Manchester days.

My strength was holding together well, but then during the last race of the weekend while I was in standby position in the pit lane. For whatever reason, I chose to look at some pictures on my mobile, pictures of Dad... I could feel the tears coming; something within was struggling. I turned to Pete and said "Pete, I'm unravelling!" it was the only way I could explain it.

"Hang on Scott, we've nearly done for the day, just hang on" said Pete.

He was right: I could do this. And I did, I pulled myself together enough to get through the rest of it. Finish the races, put the cars away and get out of there. Pete elected to drive back, which was our usual way as I tended to be really knackered after a long day and if we had done lots of laps.

As we drove out of the gates of the track to make our way home again, it was like a switch, I sat in the passenger seat and cried to myself. Pete said nothing and just drove. I eventually fell asleep.

Two weeks later the funeral was due. But first, we had the task of choosing a coffin for dad... Jesus, that was something else again. We went to the funeral directors in Gerrard's Cross and sat with a very nice lady who had the unpleasant task of filling out the forms. It's strange, but we knew why we were there, but still as we sat there as impassive as possible, it still felt surreal and like a bad dream.

Then the time came for the lady to bring out a large catalogue that had everything you needed for a funeral in different styles. She turned the pages to the coffins section. I don't know about Karen and Bella, but I was starting to slightly freak out inside my head... We shuffled forward to look closer at the pages. All I could see was the worst parts of an Argos catalogue. All the pages were laminated too. And if you can't work out why that was, I'm sorry, but I am not going to explain it. But I had another strange thought in my head, and I felt I needed to lighten the mood.

I looked at the book feeling just as bemused as I'm sure Karen and Bella did. "Erm... ok so how much money are we going to burn here?" I felt myself say, as we all knew it was going to be a cremation. Lucky for me, everyone had a little giggle at that, and did lighten things a little. Thank god. Once all the formalities were done, we went our separate ways.

The following days there was still other plans to finalise, like the funeral venue and organising the celebration of his life at the club. So, we met up again at a garden of remembrance venue, again not too far away, and the three of us went along to the beautiful wooded area with a nice chapel-like building. We all agreed this was the perfect place for close friends and family to congregate and give him a good send-off before we moved on for a family attendance only cremation. And then later on in the evening to Strings for a celebration of his life doo with family and lots of friends.

But before that we had to go back to the director's again to place personal effects in the coffin with dad. We took it in turns to go in the room, so I have no idea what Bella and Karen put in or did while in there. But for me, I was struck with how unlike dad the room was decorated, together with a cross above the coffin on the wall. He wasn't at all religious.

He was laid with eyes closed in the box in the suit that we chose. The room had candles and felt cool. I couldn't quite get my breath for a bit. I just wanted him to start breathing again and sit up. But instead nothing happened. I opened the bag I had with me and took out the things I had brought. My daughter had drawn a picture of him. It was a portrait of him in a leopard print jacket smiling, she had done a great job. I laid it beside him in the coffin. Next a paperback book of

"Robinson Crusoe" which was from my son, and one of dad's favourite books when he was a kid. I also had a small gold coloured broach in the shape of a heart. It was from my mum, I tucked into his breast pocket. I put in one of the gold String-fellows tie pin butterflies. I knew he would want a piece of the club to go with him. It was emotionally incredibly hard.

We left and went our separate ways. The worst day was yet to come...

How a day can feel like the longest, yet shortest I didn't know could happen, until the day of the funeral.

I drove to dad's house with Sophy and the kids, where we parked my car up, as we were going to take dad's car follow-ing the hearse and other car that had Bella and her parents in. The kids were staying at a friend's house, Bella had wisely made the day easier for her and the kids who were both under 6 years old. The coffin arrived at the house in the hearse, and at the door, we all just stood and could not comprehend what we were going through. My sister Karen just stood at the door repeating over and over "This isn't happening, this isn't happening, this isn't happening."

She wasn't having a breakdown, she was just voicing exact-ly what we were all thinking, I guess. We all got in the cars and moved off. It had been a long time since I had been part of a funeral procession. And then I hated that we were going slowly, but then that's just the racing driver in me and also wanting to get this all over with. We arrived to find the place had its car park full. There were select friends who were in-vited to attend, and maybe with the odd exception... everyone came.

When we got out of the car, the fog in my mind was really starting to descend. I knew there were people there I knew and had met with dad over the years, but I really wasn't taking it all in. We went in a procession following dad to

Tchaikovsky's 1812 overture. Which for a man who was crazy about music from the sixties, would have been a surprise to a lot of people. But if you listen to it, it's perfect. He always did like a big entrance.

I'm not going to go into any detail about the whole service. Just that Karen, Bella and I each did a eulogy that we all found incredibly hard. One of my dad's long-time friends also said a few words. Then the Beatles song "Please, Please Me!" was played at some point in the service, as he always credited the Beatles for helping him get known in the club world, purely off the back of booking them just as that song hit the top of the charts and helped him have a packed house.

We left the building to Frank Sinatra's "I Did it My Way" and a spontaneous round of applause broke out as we left. Which was very moving. As we escorted him to the car and watched him being put in, I turned around to see everyone else stood out front a respectful distance from us. Out from the crowd a man walked towards me with his hands held out, I nearly had a heart attack because as I was not a hundred percent with it, for a second, I thought it was my dad, because he dressed similarly, and had long flowing grey hair, and enough of a tan to look healthy without straying to looking orange.

I realised it was Jess Conrad, the actor and singer. I quickly rallied myself so as not to look too shocked. He said... something, I can't remember what. But it was a surreal moment, add to that I had not seen Jess for something like thirty years.

We eventually headed off for the private cremation for family only. I am not going to describe that experience.

***

In the evening, after we had gone back to our homes to get changed for the celebration of dad's life, we had time to have a bit of quiet time.

I still had Dad's car, and we, Sophy and the kids headed off into London. We parked the car right out front on the taxi rank space... I defied anyone to tell us to move it. This was a night for dad. When we walked in, the place was packed... It was like the Stringfellows of old, when we were the best disco in town, and everyone wanted to be seen in there. It was a great start to remember dad.

The place was teeming with well-known people from the past heyday of the club. I said hello to a lot of people and quite a few who I'd not seen for years. We sat in the restaurant for a while when suddenly I remembered that downstairs in the office, hanging on the wall was a picture of my dad that had been made by a guy whom I really didn't like, it was an awful picture. Made my dad look truly terrible.

I left the table and went to the office to take that stupid picture off the wall, and hid it away... The hard times were just beginning, but I didn't know how hard, but taking that horrendous picture masquerading as art down, was a small satisfaction at the time.

It was a great night, and my kids loved seeing people that they recognised. But at 9 p.m. we had to leave, it was our normal opening time, and I needed to get the kids out as they were both under 18 years old. I wasn't bothered, to be honest. It was perfect timing; the whole day had been one long emotional roller-coaster.

After that, life needed to move on.

Personally, I struggled for quite a while, I was having good and bad days, but mostly bad days... After my period of compassionate leave from work came to an end, I tried to get back into it. But I found it incredibly hard for the first few months, I had been spending six months of my life, leaving a gap for being at the hospital watching dad slip away. Now I was in the club again, and all I could see was Dad every-

where. I always said, "He is the club, and the club is him!"
And I was finding out just how true my words were.

I was doing Oscar-winning performances at work, kidding
everyone and myself that I was doing okay. Only the racetracks were my salvation from myself. As like the race after
losing dad, I also went to a track straight after the funeral...
And again, it saved my sanity to be there.

The club life was different. I was struggling and trying to
hide it. Sometimes I just disappeared to an office that wasn't
used in the evening to escape it all. I should have taken longer to come back, but what would that achieve? It would only
prolong the agony of readjusting. I had to do something about
it. After a few close friends suggested it, I decided, when I
was ready, to look at Bereavement Counselling.

I had seen an -ologist after I had split up from my wife,
because I think I needed to, it took me a long time to open up
to someone, but in the end, I was glad I did. This was different, a different kind of personal hell. The human mind is still
pretty much misunderstood, I did think about reading things
myself, the self-help route. I knew I really wasn't going to
stick at that. I needed to see someone. I was hoping to find
someone for just one-on-one help. But I ended up seeing a
community-based group called 'Mind" in the town where I
lived.

It was to be group sessions, which I wasn't open to at first.
But I joined in and surprised myself. The sessions were hard
at first, there were about ten people in the group, with Three
of the people from the organisation sat within the large circle
that was formed. We all sat on chairs, and after introducing
ourselves to each other we went around the room explaining
who we had lost, you didn't have to say anything, but everyone, some more reluctantly than others, did.

I was guarded about saying who my dad was and tailored my answers around that. I was really unsure how they would react about having the son of a gentleman's club in their group. But I realised something in the second session... these people didn't care who my dad was, they were struggling with their own personal, painful loss. And like a lot of things in life, you find your fears are just yours and people are just... people.

I let on who he was and found the reaction was nothing like I had feared. In fact, the lady running the group reckoned it helps others to show that even from another walk of life, you can have the same feelings and fears as them. Not that I'm saying I'm above anyone. But I smashed one of my own views in the process of my healing. They were a great bunch of people, all with tragic loss in their lives. We got on well, and I found I was very vocal about a lot of things, I wasn't afraid to be part of the discussions, and when I got to the last day of the course, I felt I had really got a better grip on things, the bereavement counselling was more helpful than I thought it would ever be.

Even a few people came up to me and said how much it helped them that I was so open and voiced opinions that helped them and in turn many of them helped me to round off some of the edges that had gripped me in my loss.

I went back to work each time after a group meet and became a little less hard on myself. The only thing the group didn't do was influence anything about the club. It wasn't the same anymore. Without Dad, the soul had gone out of it, just for me anyway, the club was still a great night out, but for me, Elvis had left the building.

Well... not quite, his big king chair in the restaurant was like a security blanket to me, I would look at it and could almost see him in it. There were quite a few times I could be seen hovering behind it. And I got into a routine for a while. At 2 a.m. I would go sit in dad's chair in the restaurant and have a cup of tea.

And for a long time, I struggled with the time 4:01 a.m. I used to just hide somewhere for a bit. Crazy I know, but it affected me for quite a while.

As life moved on the firsts without dad came and went. Particularly hard was Christmas, New Year's and my birthday.

Knowing that Bella had received dads' ashes, I was to have a small amount for me to scatter somewhere special. I thought for a long time I would take them to Sheffield and maybe take them to where the Mojo club used to be. But then I had a better idea. Mallorca was where I always felt he was happiest. When he was in Mallorca, he was far more relaxed, and very much the dad I knew him to be.

I went to dad's house and Bella produced the box that his ashes came in. I was shocked to see a large purple box with a plastic bag inside that contained my dads' ashes. Bella saw the look on my face, and she said, "I know... but we organised everything and never thought about what they would put him in."

She was close to tears, and she was right, we had forgotten completely about a decent urn. But then even I didn't have the right thing to take some of the ashes away in. The best I could do was a metal drinks flask that I had. It wasn't right, but it was all I had. We opened the box, and I realised that we didn't have anything to take the ashes out with. Bella went away and came back with a big silver serving spoon. We didn't know whether to laugh or cry between us. It was a moment I will never forget because we were both on the verge of tears as I began to shake slightly as I dipped the spoon in. I found I was holding my breath.

I got it over as quickly as possible... and closed up the flask and box. We were both relieved. I headed off soon after with my flask of dad on the passenger seat. That too was surreal for me. I had spent the last year, more or less, with him in the passenger seat.

17

CLOSURE

At Peace in Mallorca

2019

Dad's ashes sat on my shelf at home in the flask until I found a better vessel online through that shop of everything called Amazon. It was a tube that was better for travelling because I planned to take the ashes to Mallorca and to scatter them in the sea in line with his villa on the hill. The cardboard tube had a nice picture of a sunset on it too, which was perfect.

The first anniversary of dad's death was a hard day, and I didn't go into work. I don't think anyone expected me to. But what I did do on that day was book a holiday for my daughter and I in Mallorca. We were going to stay with one of my old school friends who lived out there, and we had seen many times on our holidays in the past.

The holiday was planned entirely around taking my portion of dads' ashes to scatter in the sea. I got hold of some of his friends and they organised getting a boat. The whole holiday and experience were very therapeutic for me. On the day we met up with a few close friends of my dad in Port Portals. The boat that they had brought was perfect, a lovely big Sunseeker in silver. We climbed aboard with swimming gear as well as the ashes. They had brought my dad's favourite champagne, Dom Perignon and some nibbles to eat.

We arrived at the anchoring point that was as in line with his villa on the hill as we could. We waited for the boat to settle, and we filled our glasses, I made a short speech, a true story of how one day, years before while on his own boat, he dropped his sunglasses overboard, they were very expensive I was in the water at the time, but couldn't get to them quick enough and I couldn't get down to the seabed where they lay because it was a long way down. So, he dove into the water from the boat to have a go at getting them himself. He too struggled to get them, and so I made the analogy that with my help, he was going to go have another look for them. And so, on the 23rd of July 2019 I slowly tipped dad into the lovely warm waters of the Mediterranean. One of dad's friend's wife placed some flowers in the sea just where I poured him. Then after a short time of getting myself together after a lovely hug from my daughter Isabelle, I got changed into my swimming trunks and went for a last swim with dad. Isabelle did the same. We even had dive masks with a snorkel. I could still see a faint cloud of dust drifting to the bottom of the seabed. It was very emotional and uplifting at the same time. He was where he liked to be the most. My mind filled with visions of him lying in the sun on the front of his boat, looking very relaxed and enjoying life.

And that's exactly what Dad did, he worked hard to enjoy life, a lesson for us all.

Eventually, we pulled up the anchor and slowly sailed back to the harbour. It was a beautiful sunny day with the sound of the boat's engines burbling away as we cut through the water, making our way back to see what life had in store for us next. Dad would have approved. Especially about the champagne!

18

Moving On

The ashes trip was a game-changer. I felt I had done the right thing. I'm just sorry that ALL the ashes weren't there, or that Karen and Bella weren't with us. On the journey back to port, I was sat with Isabelle on the front of the boat gently cruising along. I felt so good about it all, and incredibly sad that dad's house on the hill was sold. Just because we were around there, we took a little drive up to where the Villa was. It felt strange to drive up, stop outside knowing we weren't going in. But again, it was another closure exercise for myself, I think.

We had a wonderful holiday in Mallorca, because it wasn't all about the ashes, but also a time to relax in a place I knew well. The constant emotional rollercoaster I had been on had taken its toll. I actually slept well while out there, unlike most nights at home. We went to all the restaurants and coffee shops that we had been to both with Dad and as a family unit.

One of the restaurants we went to, called La Opera, as a family we visited it every time, had also changed itself. New management had updated and taken away its family feel. That too served to teach me the lesson that everything changes... eventually. In some way it was fitting that the place we visited had now changed, as we were not a family unit these days ourselves.

It was still a fantastic experience and one that endears Mallorca so much to my heart. I'm sure I'll return many times in the future and I will make new memories that will have their own special meaning, but without the tag of dad to them. But I am sure I'll still be reminded of him in many places.

Here I am just over two years on from losing dad, and nearly a year on from the trip to Mallorca writing this very personal account of life with dad, for all those that are interested in reading. Within those two years a lot has happened. Club life was a rollercoaster on its own. The changers after became a challenge, not to mention how much the whole place was still like walking around in dad's head. Some people in the club became hard to work with, but also, I was trying to get on with my life, and sometimes not doing a very good job of it. However, I was hiding the pain of losing dad, and some people didn't get that.

There were a couple of incidences that really were overblown and, I think, designed to push me out of the club. The first one was a at the end of 2018, I was still struggling over dad, but a party was being organised for just before Christmas. All the staff were tiptoeing around me while going to the organiser of the doo who worked in the club too. It was to be held at another club, and I got wind of it... but nobody was asking me if I wanted to go.

Admittedly I was in a very sensitive way and felt the people I worked with were cutting me out. From my point of view, they didn't want me there, it was all about celebrating his life on their own terms. I thought I got on really well with all the staff, but this made me feel cut out. As if I wasn't allowed to be part of it. It all came to a head one night as I confronted the organiser. It had been building up in my head most of the night as I saw staff coming in and out of the office showing their ideas for the "doo".

I spoke up after someone else had been in and out. Actually, I went out of the room... then turned around and came back in... "So, when am I going to be told about this fucking party that everyone else is going to?" I should have been calmer, but I wasn't myself, the loss of dad was filling my head day and night, and not sleeping, so my judgement was off.

However, the organiser hit back at me, "Scott, you can't even look at a picture of your dad without getting upset, we didn't want to add to your grief." Which was a good point, but I was needing friends to help me not cut me out, which is something maybe they hadn't thought of. Likewise, I hadn't thought they were not wishing to upset me. But like many people, they didn't know me well enough. I stormed out of the office... I went to go calm down.

It wasn't too long after when Cliff Silver the 99% shareholder and owner turned up at the club, which was rare, as he generally only came in at night to have dinner with bankers and not really a night kind of man. He was in the area apparently, and soon I was summoned by him to go to the office.

The organiser of the party was there and had evidently called him on the phone to complain that I had yelled and sworn at her. In the office, I explained I hadn't sworn directly at her, just that there was a party and I was aggrieved about not being told of or thought of that I might want to go, but that also I'd like to at least to have been asked.

I apologised to her if she thought I was swearing at her, but I was just pissed off at all the secrecy. Cliff, who was sitting nearby, suddenly said he was going to have to suspend me! For what? Being upset at being cut out? At that point, the organiser realised how fast this whole stupid thing was moving and said to Cliff, "I don't think it needs to come to that, I accept his apology." Basically, she could see that He was going to possibly use this against me.

Maybe she also saw the bigger picture. Whatever, we sorted it out between us. And he left the room. The party went ahead, I didn't go, but I saw the short video clips on social media... And yes, I would like to have gone, as all the people in the video were the staff I knew well and worked with. It hurt a bit all truth be told but served to remind me that regardless how I felt about the people I worked with; they didn't feel the same about me.

The other one was far more serious, but still stupid. My father's old PA Pat Jay wanted to come into the club to see me, together with her friend and also dad's book co-writer Fiona. They were just coming in to see me. Not to talk about the club or Cliff, reason being that Pat had signed a non-disclosure agreement as part of her redundancy. When they arrived, I put their names on my guest list, and in hindsight I shouldn't have done it. But I put different names down. Mainly because I knew Cliff didn't like them.

He had made dad's PA redundant, he even said to her, "No Peter, no job," which was a heartless thing to say. As for Fiona, she was a dangerous writer in his eyes. I thought it was the best thing to do at the time. I should have put their real names and be done with it. We had a nice night and talked about anything but the club or anything related to it other than dad stories.

After they had gone, the night progressed as normal. But at some point, I got an email from Cliff. It was full of angry words about letting Pat and Fiona in the club as they were banned, which I didn't know. But didn't think it would be a problem. It was a knee jerk reaction from Cliff as he was afraid of what could be said.

This went on for quite a while though the evening, even when I drove home at 5 a.m. the emails built up to when I got home where I sat in the car in my parking space and read through everything before going in. I was amazed at the big fuss over nothing. Again, I didn't think about where this was leading.

The next evening at work I was summoned into an office. The back office this time, which meant it was a hearing for an investigation. The GM asked questions and I answered truthfully. Then the next phase came, another meeting, this time with the Senior club Director Julian Russell, which was more like a kangaroo court complete with a veiled threat at the end. The whole thing was quietly dropped without an outcome, other than "the incident will be kept on file for a year," and I lost my food privileges.

I was made to not have whatever I wanted off the menu and instead have the staff meals on offer on the night, which made life a little tough for me as I get problems with diverticulitis which is a digestive illness that I have to manage and meals presented to me were not always going to work for me. This went to prove to me it was designed to make me walk of my own volition. One night, about two weeks after, I checked the reception computer, I found the names with BANNED written large. But I doubted when it was added. And sure enough a day or two later I saw the day receptionist and asked her when she updated the info about Pat and Fiona. She said, "about a couple of days ago, err... about two weeks ago... or two months."

My curiosity satisfied, I said, "thank you for that' and walked out of the reception. I didn't mention it to anyone else, but I knew where I stood now. I get where Cliff was coming from, but at the same time he was being paranoid, and they only came to see me. I feel I was treated pretty badly through it all. And it didn't end there, I brought my son in the club for his 18th birthday, just him and I. I was told I could not put it on the club, and I had a limit on my drinks allowance.

But it was free cocktails night up to 12 a.m. So, I got my son whatever he wanted, of which he had two drinks, and I had one. But I was still charged! It was ridiculous in my own opinion. The club was my family legacy and looked to me like I was being persecuted at any chance.

Since all that, things have changed again, Cliff, the major shareholder has sold his shares, without informing Karen, Bella or I beforehand, but sold them to what turns out to be the best person for the job.

I get on very well with the new owner, and the new owner is doing his best to keep the club going during these COVID times.

Outside of the club, I was not sleeping well. I have to admit dad did make life quite easy sometimes, especially if I was struggling financially. He didn't give me millions, just enough to help me out. Lucky for dad I wasn't an alcoholic or into drugs. I think all the years of helping me in my racing was more than enough.

I just wished I'd managed to reach my goal after all his help to repay his generosity. The fact I managed to say thank you to him for all his help and my racing years, while he was in hospital, was very pleasing for me, and heart breaking at the same time.

Within that time, I've also had a couple of relationships come and go. And now I'm seeing someone who, I think, might be the right person, though she lives bloody miles away up north, it seems to be working. I'm sure dad would have just rolled his eyes just at the thought of driving a long way to see someone who might be right for me. But then he made sure everyone he cared about was nearby.

He had a way of drawing people close to him, even though he treated coming to my house like a big deal and I'm only thirty minutes away. But he thought nothing of jumping on a plane, from Gatwick of all places, even though Heathrow was closer to him, and he would happily be on a flight for two hours to get himself to Mallorca. So there was a degree of a selfish streak, he did kind of expect everyone else to go to him or he would assume the leader's role with everything.

Well, everything except things he had little interest in. But you'll find that with a lot of people who are the boss of their own company.

Currently, we are in the middle of a world pandemic. We are in lockdown, and it's like trying retirement before you need to. It could also kill the club if it goes on for too long. I'm not sure how dad would have dealt with this, and I'm kind of glad he's not around to deal with it. As we have had to make staff redundant, and Dad would have hated having to do that.

Regardless of what the press or people that don't agree with the kind of club we are thought of my Dad, I knew him as he was, a kind, intelligent, helpful, caring and loving father. Who also had his faults, but he also admitted when he was wrong. He knew how to make his clubs work well, he was entertaining and charismatic though a little stern at times. His mind never stopped about the club.

We lost him at age 77. This year (2020) on 17th of October he would have been 80 years old, if it hadn't been for cancer, I think he would have made it well into his 80's as his own father made it to 83.

I'm going to miss him forever, but not let it pull me down. He was an inspiration and certainly didn't let setbacks hold him back. I have so many happy memories with him, most of which are here, but I know there are many more that just didn't come to the surface of my mind while writing. Those memories will need jogging by others.

I can't say I'm over losing dad, because I still have the odd bad day and I just get myself past it the best I can. The counselling I had was very helpful, and I can still talk to my mum on the phone. I can even still talk to my ex-wife because she understands having lost her own father last year, and her mother the same year she gave birth to our daughter. Only those that go through the same thing can truly understand the bad days.

Right now, I have no idea what the future holds for me, or the club for that matter. It's true to say that Stringfellows isn't the same without Dad. But I hope whatever happens, my Dad is proud of what I do next as I was always proud of his achievements. I'm seriously considering going into writing. I've been writing a few stories, and I would like to see if I have what it takes.

My dad has been described as a legend, and I know he liked that. He left his mark in the world and though there won't be a statue to celebrate the life of a great name in nightclubs. He will be remembered by so many people who loved his venues.

I, on the other hand, am blessed with many wonderful memories, video footage, and so many pictures. But mainly the visions in my head that replay from time to time are fondly welcomed, though sometimes still catch me out.

I find it strange that more often than not, it isn't moments with other famous people, or club encounters, or even track related memories that come to mind. It's the everyday normal stuff. How whenever we walked together on a street, he would put his hand on the back of my neck, almost like an arm across my shoulder, and not in an aggressive way, just relaxed. I'm really going to miss that.

Or sometimes he would shout from his office or lounge in whichever house "Scotty... make us a coffee would you please?" I can still hear that in my mind from time to time, or the sound of a motorboat at the harbour in Mallorca. Whenever I put sun cream on when the weather is hot, the smell of that, particularly Nivea cream, they all remind me of him.

I've been told I have some mannerisms like him and when I fall asleep in a chair in front of the TV, my head goes back, and my mouth drops open... just like he used to.

I had 52 years with him, and all of them were wonderful years. I don't think I could have asked for a better Dad. He really was as the saying goes "One in a Million". But on today's scale, he was "one in 7 Billion".

The End... of this life story at least.

ABOUT THE AUTHOR

Scott was born in 1966 to Peter and Coral Stringfellow. Their young family moved around the north of England a lot as Peter, a nightclub owner, developed his business. As a result, Scott went to schools in Wakefield, Leeds, Manchester and London.

Scott's original plan was either to be a club DJ or an actor, even though from an early age he also had dreams of becoming a racing driver. When acting didn't pan out, he worked for his father Peter in the Hippodrome night club and learned to be a lighting technician. Soon an opportunity presented itself and he managed to turn his racing dream into a reality.

He raced cars in FF1600 starting in 1984, winning two championshps in 1986 before moving up to British Formula 3 in 1987 where he contested the Class B section for three years running. In later years of his racing he moved into being a motor racing instructor, working for many schools and track day companies as well as manufacturer days. After twenty one years as an instructor, he decided to make a major change and went back to working in his father's night clubs. Within a few short years he became club director.

For the next 11 years Scott worked the nightlife. When his father passed away in 2018, he began to write about the life he had with his dad, which at first was his way of dealing with the pain of losing his father. Now he hopes to develop his writing in the future and is also rediscovering his motorsport instructing roots.

ABOUT THE PUBLISHER

Two guys with extensive experience in publishing, editing, and SEO got together one afternoon and decided there were people out there with stories to tell but who needed help to bring them into the world. **Jerry Mooney** and **Troy Lambert** hammered the idea of helping others into establishing a publishing company that could offer innovative options and more than one path to publication for authors using modern technology, multimedia promotions, and the power of **print on demand** publishing.

Several months into the project, their company, **Unbound Publishing, LLC of Idaho** was contacted by **Rick Mayston** of **Agent Fox Media, London**. He proposed joining forces in a new venture to offer authors in the UK an alternative to the expense and risk of set print by applying the use of modern technology, multimedia promotions and multiple platforms **beyond the book**. These include gallery exhibitions, art, photos, music, and media appearances.

As a part of our partnership we are able to offer unique promotional opportunities including the **Agent Fox Media** YouTube program **"In the Fox's Den."** Not only is this a great media asset for authors, but it's shared across all social media platforms and distributed worldwide. This helps these great authors get the attention they deserve.

What started with a shared vision and a belief that authors deserve better brings us where we are today. The collaborative, post-Brexit, trans-Atlantic partnership formed in the middle of a global pandemic aims to give authors a voice, storytellers a chance to shine, and all under a hybrid, print on demand model that operates with a new kind of efficiency. **Print on demand** and modern tools enable us to produce products of the same or higher quality than publishers with set print runs are able to or willing to do. This makes books and media more profitable for both the publisher and the author.

The team includes **Rick and Beverley Mayston of Agent Fox Media, London**. **Jerry Mooney and Troy Lambert** are the co-founders of Unbound Publishing, LLC of Idaho, United States. We also thank our cover designer, **Mick Mamuzelos**, our editors **Dana Long and Jon Olsen**, proofreaders, formatters, and other members of both teams too countless to name here.

Want to keep up to date with what we are publishing next? Subscribe to our newsletter and check out the other books published under our partnership and published by **Unbound Publishing** by visiting our website, unboundpublish.com.

Are you a storyteller who wants to become an author? Your ideas, your story, could change the world, and we want to give you the best opportunity to do just that. Contact us today! If you're based in the UK, get in touch with **Rick** and **Agent Fox Media** at rick@agentfoxmedia.com and if you are in the US, email info@unboundpublish.com.

"Where storytellers become authors, and authors find the success they deserve."

Lightning Source UK Ltd.
Milton Keynes UK
UKHW021103021120
372650UK00017B/1171/J